CHRIS KING

The Beginner's Guide To Coaching Kids Soccer (Ages 5 to 10)

A Complete Resource For Parents And Volunteers – From First Practice To Game Day

Copyright © 2025 by Chris King

All rights reserved. No part of this publication may be reproduced, stored or transmitted in any form or by any means, electronic, mechanical, photocopying, recording, scanning, or otherwise without written permission from the publisher. It is illegal to copy this book, post it to a website, or distribute it by any other means without permission.

First edition

This book was professionally typeset on Reedsy.
Find out more at reedsy.com

Contents

1. INTRODUCTION - THE BEGINNER'S GUIDE TO COACHING KIDS SOCCER — 1
2. GETTING STARTED AS A SOCCER COACH — 4
3. HANDLING COMMON CHALLENGES WHEN COACHING A KIDS SOCCER TEAM — 24
4. ESSENTIAL SOCCER COACHING EQUIPMENT — 34
5. PLANNING AND RUNNING TRAINING SESSIONS — 38
6. FUNDAMENTAL SOCCER SKILLS — 49
7. BEYOND THE BALL: DEVELOPING PERCEPTION AND DECISION MAKING… — 73
8. EIGHT TRAINING SESSION PLANS — 79
9. TIPS FOR COACHING A BEGINNER GOALKEEPER IN SOCCER — 116
10. BASIC UNDERSTANDING OF KIDS SOCCER RULES AND GUIDELINES — 121
11. GAME DAY ESSENTIALS — 124
12. FORMATIONS FOR KIDS SOCCER TEAMS (BY AGE GROUP) — 135
13. BUILDING TEAM SPIRIT AND CONFIDENCE — 138
14. PARENT AND VOLUNTEER ENGAGEMENT — 145
15. AGE APPROPRIATE COACHING TECHNIQUES — 153
16. MASTER SOCCER SKILLS AT HOME — 169
17. END OF SEASON WRAP UP AND REFLECTION — 180
18. OTHER SOCCER BOOKS, COURSES AND PODCASTS BY CHRIS KING — 185
19. THE IMPORTANCE OF PLAY AND CREATIVITY — 187
20. PLAYER DEVELOPMENT AND LONG-TERM GROWTH — 191
21. FINAL THOUGHTS — 194

1

INTRODUCTION - THE BEGINNER'S GUIDE TO COACHING KIDS SOCCER

THE BEGINNER'S GUIDE TO COACHING KIDS SOCCER
A Complete Resource For Parents And Volunteers
- From First Practice To Game Day -

- **Special Offer – Online Kids Coaching Course**

As a reader of this book, you can get my *Coaching Kids Soccer* course on Udemy at a discounted price. Use this link to access the discount: https://rebrand.ly/kidscourse (or head to my website and use the direct link)

- If you find this guide helpful, be sure to check out **Coaching Kids Soccer Volumes 1, 2, and 3** — available in both eBook and paperback.

- For free soccer drills, coaching tips, and resources, visit: chriskingsoccercoach.com

THE BEGINNER'S GUIDE TO COACHING KIDS SOCCER

Hi, I'm Chris King – Welcome to your guide to coaching kids' soccer!

I've played soccer since I was five and I've coached children and adult teams at grassroots level in both the United Kingdom and Australia for the last fifteen years, completing coaching courses along the way.

This book will lead you through everything you need to know to become a grassroots soccer coach – from planning your first practice to game day.

Coaching young players is a rewarding experience, but it can also feel overwhelming at first. **This book is here to break things down into simple, easy-to-follow steps** so you can focus on what matters most—helping kids learn and have fun.

Whether you're a parent stepping up to help your child's team, a volunteer that is keen to help their club, or someone completely new to coaching (No experience? No problem!), this book will provide you with the tools, strategies, and confidence you need to get started.

Children's soccer is about far more than just winning matches. At this developmental stage, the focus should be on building basic skills, fostering teamwork, and creating positive experiences on the field.

Kids need encouragement, patience, and an environment where mistakes are seen as part of the learning process. As a coach, you can shape their relationship with the game—whether it becomes a lifelong passion or just a fun childhood memory depends largely on the experience you create.

This book has lots of great information that will make your life easier as a kids soccer coach. From running your first training session to managing game day, you'll find practical tips, age-appropriate drills, and strategies for player development.

Here are the chapters that will help you become a kids soccer coach!

1. **Introduction – The Beginner's Guide To Coaching Kids Soccer**
2. **Getting Started As A Soccer Coach**
3. **Handling Common Challenges When Coaching A Kids Soccer Team**
4. **Essential Soccer Coaching Equipment**
5. **Planning And Running Training Sessions**
6. **Fundamental Soccer Skills**
7. **Beyond The Ball: Developing Perception And Decision Making In Young Soccer Players**
8. **Eight Training Session Plans**
9. **Tips For Coaching A Beginner Goalkeeper In Soccer**
10. **Basic Understanding Of Kids Soccer Rules And Guidelines**
11. **Game Day Essentials**
12. **Formations For Kids Soccer Teams (By Age Group)**
13. **Building Team Spirit And Confidence**
14. **Parent And Volunteer Engagement**
15. **Age Appropriate Coaching Techniques**
16. **Master Soccer Skills At Home**
17. **End Of Season Wrap Up And Reflection**
18. **Other Soccer Books, Courses And Podcasts By Chris King**
19. **The Importance Of Play And Creativity**
20. **Player Development And Long-Term Growth**
21. **Final Thoughts**

Whether you're teaching the fundamentals of dribbling or coaching on game day, remember: your role as a coach is not just about soccer—it's about mentoring, inspiring, and making sure every child has fun!

Let's go!
   Chris King

2

GETTING STARTED AS A SOCCER COACH

Topics covered in "GETTING STARTED AS A SOCCER COACH"

1. **Overview Of The Role Of A Kids Soccer Coach**
2. **Coaches (You!) Personal Preparation**

Starting your journey as a kids' soccer coach can feel overwhelming - especially if you don't know much about soccer! This guide will help you get started and make sure you (and the team you're coaching) have a fun and enjoyable experience.

You will learn the main things that are required of a kids soccer coach, how to plan training sessions, what equipment you'll need, plus some of the rules and guidelines of kids soccer aged 5 to 10.

I will go into more detail on specific topics in other chapters, but this chapter is aimed at giving you an overview of some of the main things to expect as a coach and some general tips.

1. OVERVIEW OF THE ROLE OF A KIDS SOCCER COACH

Being a kids' soccer coach is much more than teaching soccer skills. You're also a motivator and organiser.

Here are some of the main things you will be doing as a kids soccer coach:

1. Teaching Fundamental Skills:
   Your main job is to introduce children to the basic skills and rules of soccer – while making sure the experience is fun and accessible for all.

You can do this by focussing on simple, age-appropriate concepts.

For kids aged 5 to 10, the key is to start with the basics. Teach them how to dribble, pass, and shoot *in straightforward terms.*

For instance, you can explain dribbling as "keeping the ball close to your feet while moving" or describe passing as "aiming the ball to a teammate using the inside of your foot." Keep the language simple.

Use visual cues or props, like demonstrating dribbling with a cone to represent a defender that you can dribble around.

Also use metaphors: **Describe dribbling as "keeping the ball on a leash" to encourage control**. Chances are they have walked a dog before so they know that a leash keeps the dog under control and they can therefore relate it back to dribbling.

2. Instil a love for the game:
   Kids won't always get the technique right, but that's okay. Encourage them to laugh off mistakes and try again. The focus at this age should be on building confidence and having fun.

Set small, achievable goals, like **"In pairs, see how many times you can pass back and forth in a minute."**

Introduce "magic moments"—celebrate when a player does something new or improves noticeably. Give them a compliment ("Awesome job dribbling!") or a high five!

Create end of training mini-tournaments or fun awards to leave kids excited for the next practice.

3. Encourage Team Spirit:
You'll play a key role in teaching kids how to work together, communicate, and support one another.

4. Celebrate group achievements:
Create opportunities to highlight team successes, like great passing sequences or teamwork leading to a goal. Avoid singling out players unless it's to praise effort or sportsmanship.

Example: After a match, you might say, "I loved how you all worked together to pass the ball around today—great teamwork!"

During practice, introduce exercises that require collaboration, like passing relays or group goal challenges ("Can we make 5 passes in a row as a team?").

5. Model good sportsmanship:
Show kids how to respect their opponents, referees, and teammates. This can include shaking hands after a game or praising an opponent for a good play.

Role-play situations at training where kids can practice phrases like "Good try!" or "Nice pass!".

Address negative behaviours like arguing or blaming teammates by turning them into teachable moments. For example, "What could we say instead of blaming?" The answer here if a child has blamed a teammate for not passing them the ball may be "Try to get your head up so see if there is a teammate in a better position".

6. Managing Logistics:

Behind every great session and season is planning! Unfortunately being a soccer coach isn't just about teaching your kids how to do a Cruyff turn. Organisation is a big part and it helps you enjoy being a soccer coach a lot more.

I'll delve deeper into this in later chapters. But here's a tip to help you stay ahead and be organised (which will in turn help you and your players enjoy the season)!

Organise training and game times and communicate with parents: Use a group messaging app to inform parents of practice times, game locations, and any changes. Communication builds trust with the parents.

Example 1: Send a weekly/bi-weekly message with a brief overview of the upcoming session's focus and any items kids need to bring.

Post reminders of positive behaviours or "skill of the week" challenges in your updates. This could be a message as simple as "At Tuesdays training session we will be working on dribbling, with a focus on players non-preferred foot". This way, parents can encourage their child to practice dribbling using both feet in the lead up to the training session.

Example 2: Send a message at the start of the week which includes the game location and kick off time. Get confirmation of the availability of your players. This way you can make sure that you have enough players and parents can make arrangements to get children to the game - carpooling if needed.

7. Create a safe and inclusive environment:

Take time to learn each player's name and make sure everyone gets equal playing time during games. **Include activities for various skill levels so no child feels left out.**

For example, during drills, at different stages **do both** of the following:

- Pair more experienced players with beginners to encourage peer learning.
- Pair players of the same level with each other so they don't feel pressured, plus the more developed players can push each other to improve.

Rotate players frequently to ensure everyone has a chance to play with and against different peers. Different players are motivated by different challenges.

8. Plan ahead:

At training, always have a backup drill or activity ready. If one exercise isn't working, switch to another to keep the kids engaged. Preparation is key to running smooth sessions!

Example: Keep a list of games that take little or no setting up, like "Red Light, Green Light". Games like this can refocus attention and energy.

Note: "Red Light, Green Light" is a simple game where each child has a ball and is in a line across the field or dribbling in an area. The coach calls out "Green Light!" and players start dribbling quickly.

When the coach calls "Red Light!" the players stop, placing their foot on top of the ball. It helps with dribbling skills, keeping close control and listening to instructions. You can add extra rules such as 'Orange light' (slow dribbling), 'first gear', 'second gear', etc to make the kids dribble faster and also 'reverse' to help them work on their turns. This drill doesn't require any setting up or equipment so it can be done anywhere.

2. Coaches (You!) Personal Preparation:

Learn youth soccer rules: Spend time reviewing your league's rules. Understanding guidelines like field sizes, game durations, and specific rules for your age group will save you being surprised

Highlight any, younger "kid-specific" rules, like allowing kick-ins instead of throw-ins. This way you can use the same rules during practice.

These league rules can usually be found with a quick Google search. But to give you an idea, here are some of the main regulations for an Under 7/8's Football league.

You will find that most of these rules are fairly standard across most countries.

- **Format** 5v5
- **Match Length** 20 mins each way.
- **Pitch Size** 40 yd x 30 yd
- **Ball Size** 3
- **Substitutions** Roll-off roll-on substitutions (also called interchange) can be made at any time during the game with permission from the referee, including players who have already been substituted.
- **Throw-ins** Traditional throw-ins are part of the rules, but referees may allow players to try again if they use incorrect technique.
- **Offside** There is no offside.
- **Playing Equipment** Shin pads are mandatory. These should be covered entirely by knee-length socks.

3. Plan sessions in advance:

Create a simple outline for each practice. I usually divide it into warm-up, drills, and game. Include fun activities to keep kids excited.

For younger kids, use themes like "Pirates vs. Ninjas" "Sharks vs Surfers" to make drills more engaging. Also, I find kids love it when I use animals . For example "Now dribble as fast as a cheetah!" "Slow down to a turtle's pace".

I like to use the below format for my kids training sessions (I expand on this in more details in my "Coaching Kids Soccer Volumes 1,2,3" book which is available on Amazon).

Please note: If you have players that need to work on practising a skill, simply change either Part 1 or Part 3 (a small sided game) to dedicating it to skill practise.

TRAINING SESSION PLAN DATE 1.2.23

FOCUS OF SESSION
DRIBBLING

1 SMALL SIDED GAME
___4v4___

2 FUN SOCCER GAME
___GATES___

3 SMALL SIDED GAME
4v4 : REWARD DRIBBLING
ENCOURAGE SKILL BEING WORKED ON
(IE PASSING, DRIBBLING, SHOOTING, 1v1)

4 FUN SOCCER GAME
___SIMON SAYS___

5 SMALL SIDED GAME
___4v4___

- **I break my session into 5 equal parts.** If it is an hour session, this allows 10 minutes for each part and a spare 10 minutes for talking, drink breaks, changing drills etc.
- **I pick a topic for the session** ("Dribbling" in the example training session plan.
- **Parts 1,3 and 5 are simply small sided games** (3v3,4v4, etc in a small area with goals at each end). Part 3 encourages a focus on the skill of the session in a game situation. Do this by using encouraging words, giving high fives when the skill is performed, awarding double points/goals if the skill of the session leads to a goal, etc.
- **Parts 2 and 4 are fun soccer games that help the players work on the main focus of the session.** Those two games are "Gates" and "Simon Says" in the example.

To summarise the session plan:

- The session focus is on dribbling.
- **The first part** of the session is simply a small sided game.
- **The second part** is a fun soccer based game to work on the main skill (dribbling), in this example "Gates".
- **The third part** is another small sided game. This time with rewarding players who use the skill. (I might make a rule that if a player dribbles and then makes a nice pass or scores a goal, it is worth double).
- **The fourth part** is another fun soccer based game to work on the main skill (dribbling), in this example "Simon Says".
- **The fifth part** is another small sided game. I let the kids just play and enjoy themselves without interfering much at all – just encourage!

4. Arrive early:

Being early allows you to set up equipment and greet kids and parents as they arrive. This makes a great first impression and sets a welcoming tone. Give the kids a smile plus a high five as they arrive (and use their names)!

If a few kids have arrived early, use this time to set up a small game so they get extra time playing soccer and therefore touches on the ball. Parents can join in to make up numbers.

5. Organisational Tools:

Use a notebook or app to plan your sessions. Even if you only refer to it before training, it helps crystallise what you will be doing for that session. Plus you will be reusing training sessions (you don't have to reinvent the wheel and make a magical new training session every time through out the season). So by keeping previous sessions in a notebook or app you can refer back to them and use them again, saving yourself time.

Plus children like routines, so you'll see them get excited if you use a game that they love.

Also make a note of which players attend each session in your notepad or app. This helps you follow up with absent players if needed.

Give "star player" stickers or stamps for those players that attend every session. These can be found on Amazon or Etsy - simply search "Soccer stickers".

6. Transporting gear:

A large sports bag with compartments keeps everything organised and is easy to carry. Have a checklist to ensure nothing is forgotten (especially in the early weeks when you are just learning). Bibs - check! Cones - check! Pop up goals - Check! Whistle - check! Fun attitude - check! Hands for high fiving - check!

Create a "coach-in-training" role for a child to help pack up equipment. It teaches children good habits and shows that gear doesn't get packed up by itself —they'll feel helpful and special.

7. First-aid kit and extras:

Always have a first-aid kit, extra water, sunscreen, spare shin pads, small towel.

Conclusion

Becoming a good soccer coach doesn't require experience—just enthusiasm, preparation, and a willingness to create a positive environment. The kids don't know (or mind) that you're not a professional coach. Remember, your primary goal is to help kids have fun and fall in love with the game. If you do this you should be proud.

Well done and have fun!

Here are some training and match day templates that you may find handy. Take a screen shot or print them out.

Or head to my website www.chriskingsoccercoach.com and download a PDF version for free that you can print out.

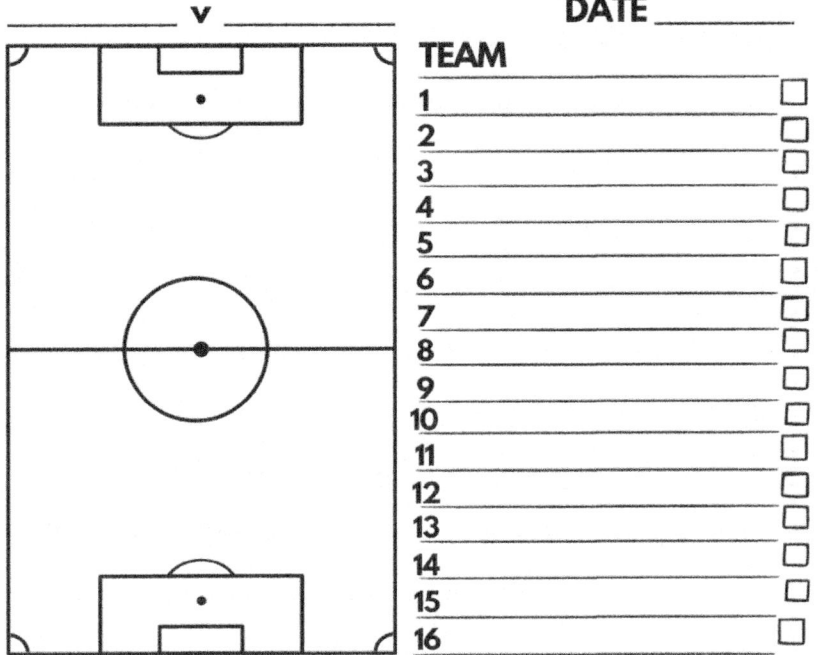

FUN SOCCER GAME 1: _____

SET UP:

PROGRESSION:

COACHES NOTES:

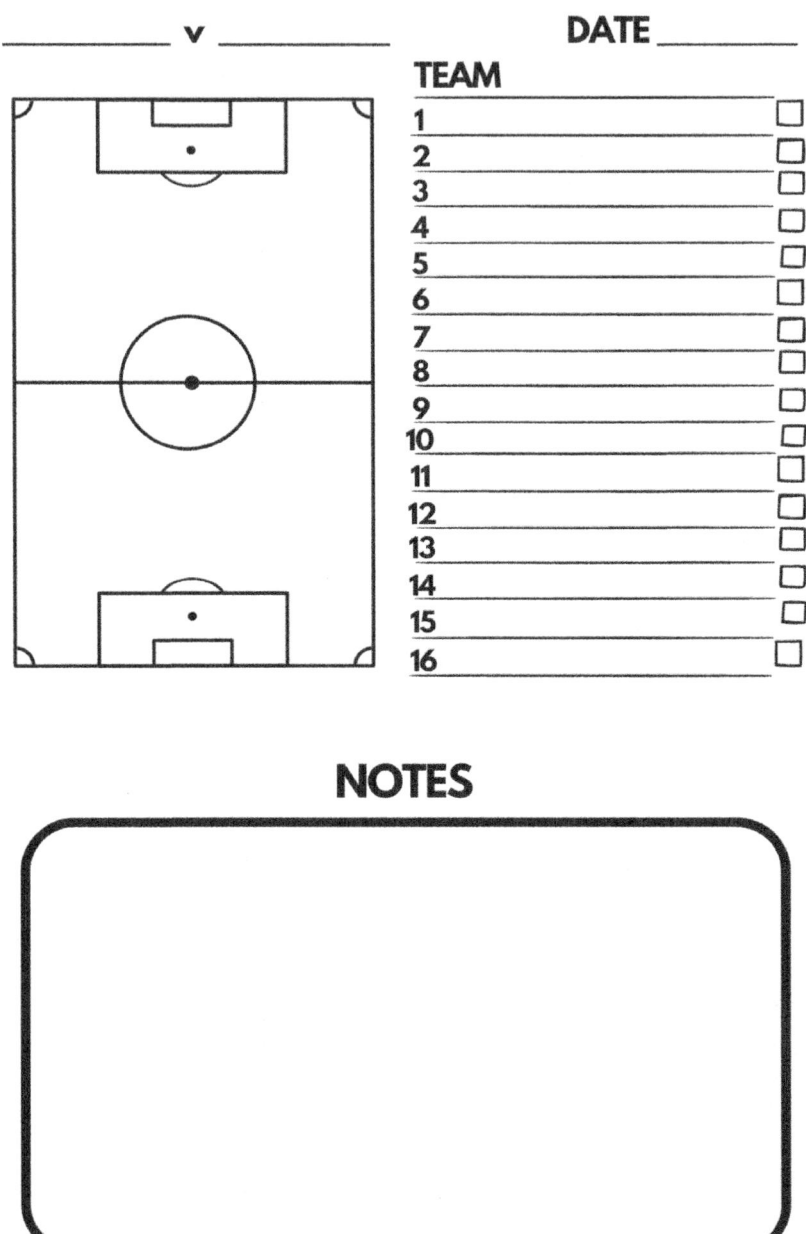

TRAINING SESSION PLAN   DATE

FOCUS OF SESSION
_____

1 — SMALL SIDED GAME
_____

2 — FUN SOCCER GAME
_____

3 — SMALL SIDED GAME
_____
ENCOURAGE SKILL BEING WORKED ON
(IE PASSING, DRIBBLING, SHOOTING, 1v1)

4 — FUN SOCCER GAME
_____

5 — SMALL SIDED GAME
_____

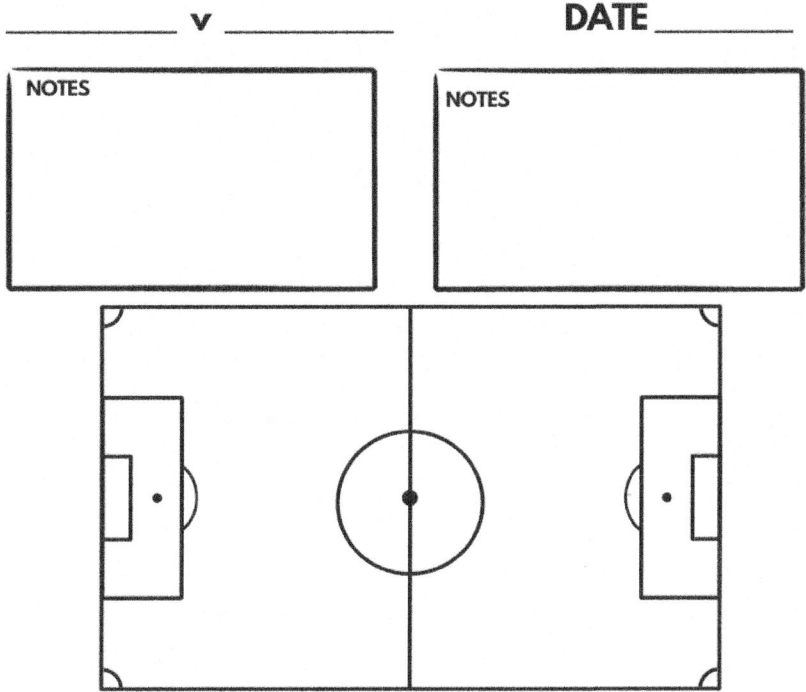

FUN SOCCER GAME 2: _____

SET UP:

PROGRESSION:

COACHES NOTES:

3

HANDLING COMMON CHALLENGES WHEN COACHING A KIDS SOCCER TEAM

Topics covered in "HANDLING COMMON CHALLENGES WHEN COACHING A KIDS SOCCER TEAM"

1. **Managing Disruptive Behaviour**
2. **Keeping Shy or Less-Confident Kids Involved**
3. **Balancing Player Abilities**

Coaching young players comes with its share of challenges. Here's how to balance different skill levels within your team, effectively manage disruptive behaviour and engage shy or less-confident players. Using these tips you can create an environment where every child feels supported and can thrive.

1. Managing Disruptive Behaviour

Coaching kids often means dealing with some disruptive behaviour, like talking too much, not listening, or general mucking around. It's important to stay calm and use these moments to teach kids about respect and teamwork. By setting clear rules and staying positive, you can help them focus and turn their energy into something fun and productive.

1. Set Clear Expectations:
   Establish team rules at the beginning of the season and reinforce them consistently.
   Example: "We listen when the coach is talking, and we respect our teammates by not interrupting."
   Tip: Create a "Team Code of Conduct" poster and review it during the first few practices and through out the season.

Additional Example: Begin each practice by reviewing one rule as a quick reminder to set the tone.
   Additional Tip: Use hand signals, like raising a hand for quiet, to quickly redirect attention without stopping the flow of practice. Another good one is "Toes! Knees! Shoulders! Head!" - call this out when you want players attention or for them to stand still. No player wants to be the last one so they get in the habit of doing it and standing still when they finish.

2. Address Disruptions Calmly:
   Avoid singling out players in front of their peers. Speak to them privately to understand the root of the behaviour.
   Example: "Hey, Shaun, I noticed you were having trouble focusing during the drill. Is something bothering you?"
   Tip: Use positive phrasing like "Let's try to focus on the next drill together," instead of "Stop messing around."

Additional Example: If a player continues disrupting, have them sit out for a few minutes with the task of observing their teammates and reporting something positive they notice.

Additional Tip: Use humour to defuse tension, like "That's some creative dribbling, but let's save the cartwheels for later!"

3. Redirect Energy:

Channel disruptive behaviour into productive activities.

Example: If a player is overly energetic, assign them a leadership role, like helping set up cones, coming up with stretches for the warm up or demonstrating a drill.

Tip: Introduce high-energy games early on like "Sharks and Minnows" to allow kids to burn off extra energy before structured drills.

4. Reward Positive Behaviour:

Recognise and praise players when they show improvement in their behaviour.

Example: "Great job staying focused today, Annie—I really appreciated your effort in the passing drill."

Tip: Use a reward system, like earning stickers or tokens for teamwork and good listening.

Additional Example: Create a "team star chart" where players earn stars for positive behaviours and team milestones. Note: If you don't want to make your own chart, a lot can be found on Etsy.

Additional Tip: At the end of practice, give shout-outs to specific players who demonstrated focus and teamwork.

5. Involve Parents if Needed:

If disruptive behaviour persists, have a respectful conversation with the player's parents to seek their support.

Example: "I've noticed Davo has been distracted during practices. Do you have any suggestions that might help us keep him engaged?"

Additional Example: Invite parents to observe a practice and provide input on strategies that might work.

Additional Tip: Frame the conversation as a partnership, focusing on how to best support the child together.

2. Keeping Shy or Less-Confident Kids Involved

Not every child will start out feeling confident on the soccer field. Some kids might hang back during drills, stay quiet, or seem unsure about joining in.

As a coach, it's important to create a safe and fun environment where every child feels included and supported. With the right encouragement and simple strategies, you can help shy or less-confident players feel like they belong and enjoy being part of the team.

1. Build Trust:
   Start with low-pressure activities to help shy players feel comfortable.
   Example: Pair them with a friendly teammate for simple passing drills.
   Tip: Use their name often to build familiarity and rapport. For instance, "Great pass, Andrew!"

Additional Example: Assign shy players small but visible tasks, like leading a line during drills, to help them feel part of the group.
   Additional Tip: Smile often and use encouraging body language to put them at ease.

2. Celebrate Small Wins:
   Highlight their efforts and progress to boost their confidence.
   Example: "That was an awesome dribble, Neil! You kept the ball so close to your feet."
   Tip: Avoid comparing them to others; instead, focus on their individual growth.

Additional Example: Give them a "personal best" moment by timing their dribbling through cones and celebrating improvements.

Additional Tip: Take videos of players performing a skill early in the season. Then show them it later in the season so they can see how far they've come.

3. Use Inclusive Drills:

Design activities where everyone contributes equally.

Example: In a "Chain Passing" game, players must pass to every teammate before scoring, ensuring everyone is involved.

Tip: Rotate roles/positions frequently so shy players have a chance to try different positions.

Additional Example: Use "keep away" games **(also know as rondos)** where there are smaller groups which ensures more touches for everyone. This could be three or four players passing a ball or dribbling a ball while one or two defenders are trying to win the ball.

> Note: I have two books on Rondos with drills you can use for children, youth or adult soccer training. Soccer Rondos Volume 1 and 2 are available on Amazon or search "Chris King Soccer Rondo" and you'll find them.

Additional Tip: Make inclusivity a team responsibility by encouraging players to cheer on every teammate, not just their best friends or the most skilled player.

Inclusive drills: Design activities where every child is involved.

For example, set up multiple stations to avoid long lines and waiting times. Long lines are a pet peeve of mine. You don't want kids waiting in line just to have one kick and then go back to the back of the line. So set up multiple stations so that waiting time is shorter. Or have players dribbling or performing a skill in the lead up to the main skill.

Add "team challenges" where groups work together to achieve a target, like scoring five goals or making 5 passes in a row.

Encouraging Participation:
   Position rotation: Allow every child to experience different roles, from goalie to striker. This keeps things fresh and helps kids develop a range of skills. At early ages kids shouldn't be pigeon holed into just one position. This is the time they should be learning different skills and positions. Versatility is a good attribute and will help children get in teams later in their footballing career.

Let kids choose their favourite position occasionally as a reward.

Celebrate effort: Highlight individual and group progress. For example, "I loved how everyone used both feet to dribble around the cones today!"
   Create a "Player of the Practice" title for standout effort or attitude, rotating it each session. When you announce the "Player of the Practice", get all the players to give them a high five or a round of applause.

4. Encourage Leadership in Small Ways:
   Give less-confident kids opportunities to lead in non-intimidating roles.
   Example: "Could you help collect the cones after this drill?" or "Can you show the group how to do a toe tap?". Little things like this go a long way in building their confidence and making them comfortable.
   Tip: Gradually increase their responsibilities as their confidence grows.

Additional Example: Let them choose a team warm-up game or call out "start" for a relay. This may seem simple but it helps give them confidence.
   Additional Tip: Praise their efforts in leadership publicly, like "Thanks, Jason, for keeping everyone organised!"

5. Create a Safe Environment:

Ensure teammates are supportive and encouraging.

Example: Remind the team to cheer each other on, like "Nice shot!" or "Great try!"

Tip: Address negative comments immediately and reinforce the importance of kindness.

Additional Example: Start (or finish) practices with a "compliment circle," where players share something positive about a teammate.

Additional Tip: Use team chants or cheers to build camaraderie and inclusivity. Does your team have a team song yet? Maybe you could have a break in the middle of training and come up with a chant together? Kids will surprise you with how inventive and funny they can be!

3. Balancing Player Abilities

Every team has players with different skill levels, from those who are confident and experienced to those who are just starting out. As a coach, your job is to create an environment where everyone can improve and feel included, regardless of their ability. By mixing up teams, tailoring drills, and encouraging teamwork, you can help all players grow while keeping practices fun and fair for everyone.

1. Group by Skill Level:

Divide players into smaller groups based on their current abilities during drills.

Example: Advanced players can practice one-touch passing while beginners focus on basic control and accuracy, using as many touches as they need.

Tip: Rotate players occasionally to ensure all players learn from each other.

Additional Example: During shooting drills, create levels where beginners aim at larger targets and advanced players aim at smaller ones. Or the beginners shoot from closer range to gain some confidence.

Additional Tip: Use coloured pinnies to distinguish groups and then you can organise drills efficiently.

2. Use Tiered Drills:

Offer varying levels of challenge within the same activity.

Example: In a shooting drill, advanced players aim for corners while others focus on simply hitting the target. Say to them before the drill to "Aim for the corners if you want to, otherwise hitting the target is just as good!"

Tip: Provide encouragement tailored to each player's level, like "Great job aiming for the target! Now let's try hitting the left side of the goal."

Additional Example: In passing drills, ask advanced players to use non-dominant feet while beginners use their dominant side.

3. Highlight Teamwork Over Individual Performance:

Design games and drills that emphasise collective success.

Example: "Passing Relay Races," where the team must complete a set number of passes and be the first to finish. I use a game where if the team scores a goal they get awarded the amount of passes they made in the lead up to the goal. For example, if a team passes three times and scores a goal they get three points (or three goals). This encourages teamwork.

Tip: Praise players for setting up their teammates, such as "That assist was fantastic, Amanda!"

4. Rotate Positions:

Allow players to experience different roles on the field to broaden their skills and confidence. This is very important at a young age.

Example: "Today, you'll try playing as a defender. Hold up and delay the attacker and focus on staying between the ball and the goal."

Tip: Use practices to identify hidden strengths, like a hesitant player excelling as a goalkeeper.

Additional Example: Rotate captains each week to give everyone a chance to lead on game day.

Additional Tip: Highlight how each position contributes to the team's overall success during feedback at the end of training.

5. Encourage Peer Support:

Pair advanced players with less experienced teammates during drills to foster mentorship.

Example: "Can you show Max how to do that step-over move you just mastered?"

Tip: Frame this as a learning opportunity for both players, emphasising teamwork.

Additional Example: Create a "buddy system" where each advanced player has a less experienced teammate to support for certain parts of training.

Additional Tip: Rotate pairings often to build relationships.

6. Celebrate Effort and Improvement:

Focus on individual progress rather than comparing players.

Example: "I've noticed how much better you've gotten at staying focused on defence, Smithy—great work!"

Tip: Use end-of-practice shout-outs to recognise effort, like "Player of the Day" for the most hustle or best sportsmanship.

Additional Example: Keep a "progress board" where players track their personal bests, like juggling records or sprint times. This can be done on your phones notes, spreadsheet or pad and pen.

Additional Tip: Celebrate milestones with certificates or fun titles like "Most Improved Dribbler."

CONCLUSION

By addressing disruptive behaviour constructively, supporting shy players, and balancing varying skill levels, you can create a team environment where every child feels valued. **With patience, encouragement, and thoughtful planning, challenges can become opportunities.**

4

ESSENTIAL SOCCER COACHING EQUIPMENT

Topics covered in "ESSENTIAL SOCCER COACHING EQUIPMENT"

1. **Essential Soccer Coaching Equipment**

Having the right gear and preparation can make all the difference to running a fun and engaging practice session. Here's what you'll need:

1. Basic Equipment:
   Soccer Balls: Size 3 for younger kids (ages 5-8) and size 4 for older kids (ages 9-10). If possible, ensure there are enough balls for each player to have one.
   Tip: Write your team or clubs initials on the balls to prevent mix-ups if there are other teams using the same area (for example, if your team is Wild Cats Under 9's, write "WC U9" on your balls).

Cones/Discs: Use cones to mark out boundaries, create goals, or drill setups. Brightly coloured cones are best for visibility (white or orange stand out the most on grass).

A couple of examples of the use of cones would be to: Create obstacle courses for dribbling practice or "gates" for passing drills where the players have to pass or dribble through two cones (the gate).

Note: Discs are handy as they are flat and don't get in the way if you need to place markers in the field of play. Sometimes cones can be frustrating for young players if they keep deflecting the ball. During passing or dribbling drills the ball hits them regularly and ricochets off in a different direction.

Goals: Portable or pop-up goals are ideal for small-sided games. If these aren't available, create goals using two cones or two poles (wider goals for younger, less skilled children, and smaller goals for older, more skilled children).

Tip: Encourage kids to take turns being "goal builders" - this simply means get them to set up the mini goals and put cones or poles out.

Pinnies/Bibs: These help distinguish teams during games.

Bibs can also be used by the coach to make sure the children get their head up during a dribbling practice. I like to tell them that at regular intervals I will hold up a coloured bib (or cone), and the first player to call out the colour of the bib gets an extra points. This encourages players to get their head up when dribbling and be aware of their surroundings.

Tip: Assign captains to distribute bibs—this is a small role that builds leadership skills.

Whistle and Stopwatch: A whistle helps grab attention quickly. Especially if there are other teams practising close by and there is lots of noise, a whistle will stand out and get your players attention. And a stopwatch keeps your drills timed and organised.

Tip: Incorporate timed challenges, like "How many passes in 30 seconds?"

Additional Useful Equipment for Training and Game Day

While not essential, the following equipment can make a better training sessions, especially for older children:

Speed Ladders and Agility Poles – Help with balance and controlled movement exercises.
Rebound Boards – Great for practising passing and ball control in a confined space.
Tactics Board – Useful for explaining formations, positioning, and team strategies.
Ball Pump – Ensures footballs are always at the correct pressure for training and matches.
Mannequins or Free-Kick Dummies – Useful for practising passing, shooting, and tactical drills.
Passing Arcs – Helps players develop accuracy and control when passing the ball along the ground.
Target Nets – Can be attached to goals to improve shooting accuracy and finishing skills.
Resistance Bands – Can be used for warm-up exercises and strength training to help prevent injuries.
Poles – Can be used to enhance dribbling and movement drills.
Adjustable Hurdles – Can be used for controlled movement drills and fitness exercises.
Foam Rollers – Helpful for post-game recovery and injury prevention.

Conclusion

Keep all you gear together so you don't forget to take anything to training. Even better if it can be stored at the club or school. Make sure to get the kids to help you pack up after training! And don't be afraid to ask parents to take it turn to wash the bibs and bring them to the next session.

If you'd like a free book, 50 TIPS ON HOW TO COACH A CHILDREN'S SOCCER TEAM - Ages 3 to 6 is available on Amazon permanently free.

Special Offer – Online Kids Coaching Course

As a reader of this book, you can get my *Coaching Kids Soccer* course on Udemy at a discounted price.

☞ Use this link to access the discount: https://rebrand.ly/kidscourse

Plus head to my website www.chriskingsoccercoach.com and enter your email for a free PDF copy of a soccer coaching book.

Thank You for Reading! *If this book has been valuable so far, please consider leaving a review on Amazon. Your feedback helps spread the word and lets other new coaches find my books.*

USA REVIEW LINK: *https://www.Amazon.com/review*
  UK REVIEW LINK: *https://www.Amazon.uk/review/create-review?&asin=B0D48YQ1DH*

5

PLANNING AND RUNNING TRAINING SESSIONS

Topics covered in "PLANNING AND RUNNING TRAINING SESSIONS"

1. **Structuring Age-Appropriate Sessions: Warm-Ups, Drills, and Cool-Downs**
2. **Keeping Kids Engaged and Focused**
3. **Adapting for Different Skill Levels**
4. **Practical Tips for Smooth Sessions**

A well-organised training session is the backbone of effective coaching. This chapter shows you how to plan and run sessions that are fun, engaging, and productive.

You will learn how to structure a session for young children that will ensure they will enjoy it and get the most out of it. This will include games and drills for the warm ups, the main session and the cool down.

Young children easily loose focus, so you will also learn tips on keeping them engaged in the session. This will help you enjoy the session as well!

And lastly, you will be coaching kids that are at different skill levels. So your role is to run a training session and coach ALL CHILDREN so they can enjoy and learn soccer together.

Let's jump into it!

1. Structuring Age-Appropriate Sessions

Young players thrive in an environment that balances learning and enjoyment. Here's how to structure your sessions effectively so kids enjoy soccer and therefore are keen to learn:

1. Start with a Warm-Up:
    Keep warm-ups simple and dynamic. Keep warm up activities short (5-10 minutes) and high-energy to get kids excited.

Incorporate light stretches and movement to prepare their muscles. Avoid static stretches; instead, use movements like high knees or arm circles.

Tip: Add a fun twist by having players mimic animal movements, like "frog jumps", "crocodile rolls" or "bear crawls." Players love to be an animal!

Example 1: At a lot of my training sessions I like to have 5 minutes of dribbling and then get straight into a game (3v3, 4v4 etc). It helps get their built up energy out straight away and all the players get plenty of touches.
    Tip: Use music during warm-ups to add energy!
    Additional Tip: Encourage kids to cheer each other on to build energy and camaraderie. Some of the things they come out with will put a smile on your face. :)

Example 2: Have a 3v3 small sided game. This makes sure that all players get lots of touches and are running around. Or use "tag" games where players dribble a ball in an area while trying to avoid being tagged by other players or the coach. This engages their minds and bodies.

Game example: Play "Sharks and Minnows." One player is the shark who dribbles and tries to tag the other players. The others are minnows dribbling their balls in or across a designated area. If tagged, they become sharks too. Keep going until there are no minnow left! Who will be the last minnow standing?

2. Focus on Core Skills:

Devote a segment of the session (or the whole session) to a specific skill, such as dribbling, passing, 1v1 or shooting. Break the skill down into simple steps.

Example: For passing, teach players to use the inside of their foot, look and aim at their target, and follow through.

Use small-sided drills that encourage frequent touches on the ball. The more touches on the ball, the sooner they will learn skills and improve.

Game Example: "Gates" where players pair up and pass through gates (pairs of cones) spread around the field.

For "Gates", set up an area with pairs of same coloured cones spread around. Then children pair up and pass the ball through the gates, counting how many they can get through in a set amount of time.

Tip: Challenge players by making the gates narrower as they improve. Or you can just have one narrow gate and the rest wider. This will challenge players but not discourage them as there are still mostly wider gates.

3. Include Fun Games:

Games related to the skill being taught make learning enjoyable. For example, if focusing on dribbling, play "Traffic Jam," where players dribble through an area littered with cones while avoiding the cones and collisions with other players. Tell the players to keep their head up as much as they can and watch for other cars! You can give them a cone to use as a steering wheel.

When playing a fun game, add small challenges, like earning a point for every successful pass, dribble or keeping the ball under control and not running into other players. See if players can get to 5 points.

Tip: Rotate roles in games to ensure all players experience different challenges. So if you are playing "Sharks and Minnows", the role of the shark is defensive (they are trying to coral players and win the ball. So make sure to swap the role so all players learn those skills).

4. End with a Small Sided Game (Scrimmage):

Small-sided games (e.g., 3v3, 4v4 or 5v5) let kids practice skills in a game. I always like to finish with a game because they get to just play and enjoy themselves. Encourage creativity and experimentation.

Example: Divide players into equal teams. If you have a large group, make sure to set up two mini-fields and split them in half. This way all the kids get more touches.

Use this time to observe and offer encouragement rather than constant correction.

2. Drills

Drills: Focus on foundational skills like dribbling, passing, shooting, 1v1 and control

After the warm up, use games like these to work on their foundational skills.

- **Example 1**: "Cones". Set up cone gates for players to practice passing with accuracy and pace. Simply pair players up and then place a pair of cones in between them to pass the ball back and forth through.
- **Tip 1:** Incorporate friendly competition, like awarding points for each

successful pass through a gate. Who can get 10 points first?

- **Example 2**: Use "Snake Dribble," where players follow a leader while keeping control of their ball. All players are moving and different dribbling speeds and skills can be practiced. For more advanced players, they can practice sole rolls, step overs, etc as they dribble.
- This is also a good game that can be used as warm up. Plus it doesn't taking any setting up!
- **Tip 2:** Rotate leaders (the head of the snake) to give everyone a chance to guide the group.

- **Example 3**: "Sharks and Surfers". Set up a square with two players without balls in the middle. Have four corners with smaller squares – these are the same areas (also called the beach) where the rest of the players start with a ball.
- The aim is for the players to go into the ocean and surf (dribble) to another corner without getting eaten (tagged) by a shark. If a player gets tagged they can become a shark or perform a simple task (10 toe taps). How many surfers can the sharks get in 2 minutes?
- **Tip 3:** Call out commands such as "left foot only!" and players must only dribble with their left foot. Or "Swap balls!" and players must swap balls and continue dribbling.

- **Example 4**: Create a "Pass and Move Square" where players form a square and pass while rotating positions. This is simple but players learn to move and not stay in the same spot after they make a pass. Plus they are passing the ball at different angles (they may be passing to the player opposite

them or to their right or left).
- **Tip 4:** Add a defender to the square to simulate game pressure. Or see how many passes they can make before the ball goes out of the square.

- **Example 5**: Organise a "Juggling Ladder," where players try to complete a certain number of juggles to progress up levels. This can be a series of squares. All players start in the first square and move on to the next square when they have completed a certain amount of juggles.
- **Tip 5:** Allow the ball to bounce once or twice in between juggles if they are just learning. And for beginners, they should start with the ball in their hands and drop it onto the ground first (or their foot) and then juggle as it bounces up.

- **Example 6**: Set up "1v1 Battles," where players try to dribble past a defender to score in a mini-goal. This helps them learn to change directions and pace to get past a defender.
- **Tip 6:** Rotate defenders frequently to keep everyone engaged.

- **Example 7**: Set up a "Follow the Leader" drill, where players mimic dribbling moves demonstrated by the coach. Players can be side by side along a line with the coach out in front so they can all see and hear the coach.
- **Tip 7:** Include simple moves like toe taps and step-overs to build confidence.

- **Example 8**: Play "Circle Passing," where players pass to teammates in a circle while calling out their names. This is a good one for early in the season if players don't know each other – plus it also helps the coach learn their names. Introduce a second ball if you think your players can handle two balls a once.
- **Tip 8:** Encourage accuracy by having players aim for their teammate's preferred foot.

- **Example 9**: Run a "Stop and Go" dribbling drill, where players alternate between fast dribbling and controlled stops.
- **Tip 9:** Use a whistle or clap to signal changes between speeds. Or animal names – Call out "Rabbit speed!", "Cow speed!", "Turtle speed!", etc.

- **Example 10**: Introduce "Dribble Cones," where kids zig zag through a line of cones spaced farther apart to focus on smooth control. Remember to tell them it's not a race. You want to see them do it correctly and only as fast as they feel comfortable.
- **Tip 10:** Encourage players to use both feet as they navigate the course.

- **Example 11**: Play "Pair Pass Through Gates," where pairs work together to pass the ball through cone gates set up around the field.
- **Tip 11:** Increase difficulty by narrowing the gates over time.

- **Example 12**: Set up a "Dribble Maze" where players navigate through cones and try to beat their time without losing the ball.

- **Tip 12:** Introduce penalties, like restarting the maze, for hitting cones to encourage precision.

If you need more kids games, pick up any of the three volumes of " Coaching Kids Soccer Volumes 1,2,3" book by Chris King, which is available on Amazon.

3. Cool-Downs:

Incorporate light jogging and stretching. For example, form a circle and have players stretch while sharing their favourite moment from the session.

Use this time for a brief reflection and positive reinforcement.

Example: Ask each player to name one thing they learned or enjoyed during practice.

Tip: End with a calming activity like "silent dribbling," where players move quietly around the field with their ball.

Additional Example: Play "Pass and Praise," where players pass in a circle and give a compliment to the person receiving the ball.

2. Keeping Kids Engaged and Focused

1. Vary Activities:

Change drills every 10-15 minutes to maintain attention. Kids can lose focus if an activity drags on.

Example: Transition from dribbling drills to a relay race involving passing.

Tip: Use a "mystery bag" containing paper with random fun tasks to keep transitions exciting. An example might be "everyone woof and act like a dog as we move onto the next drill". Or "the coach must do 5 push ups with a player on their back". Or "Guess which animal I am?".

2. Use Themes and Stories:

Engage their imagination by integrating themes. For example, during a dribbling drill, say, "Pretend you're escaping a jungle, and the cones are trees that you must dribble around to find an opening at the other end."

Create scenarios like "World Cup Finals" during small sided games to add excitement. "Welcome to this months 2025 World Cup Final, featuring teams from the Under 7 Dragons! Which players will lift the World Cup this month!"

Tip: Incorporate kids' favourite characters or superheroes into the narrative for added fun.

3. Encourage Friendly Competition:

Use games and challenges to motivate players.

Example: Divide the team into groups for a "Cone Knockdown" contest, where cones are set up around an area and players earn points for hitting cones with accurate passes.

Tip: Keep the focus on effort and improvement rather than winning.

Additional Example: Introduce a "Team Trick Challenge," where players show off a new skill and then the rest try it.

Additional Tip: Rotate groups often to prevent cliques and keep everyone involved.

4. Offer Rewards:

Celebrate effort with small rewards like stickers or "Player of the Day" titles.

Set team goals, such as completing a certain number of passes, and reward the group when they achieve it.

Tip: Use a "skill chart" in a book or app to track progress and reward milestones, like completing 10 successful juggles.

3. Adapting for Different Skill Levels

1. Group by Ability:

Create smaller groups for drills so players of similar skill levels can work together.

Example: Have advanced players practice more challenging moves like step overs, while beginners focus on basic dribbling.

Tip: Rotate groups occasionally to foster interaction and inclusivity.

2. Modify Drills:

Simplify or intensify activities based on the group's ability.

Example: For passing drills, beginners pass over short distances, while advanced players work on one-touch passes or longer distances.

Tip: Add bonus challenges, like "use your non-dominant foot," for advanced players.

3. Encourage Peer Learning:

Pair advanced players with beginners for some drills. This fosters mentorship and collaboration.

Example: Advanced players can demonstrate skills while beginners replicate them.

4. Practical Tips for Smooth Sessions

1. Prepare Ahead:

Arrive early to set up cones, goals, and other equipment. Double-check your session plan. I always like to have my session plan finalised in advance and then I can have a 5 minute review of it the night before training and on the day before I arrive at training. You always have parents and other coaches talking to you when you arrive, so make sure to review your session earlier that day as well as in the car once you arrive.

Tip: Use a checklist to ensure nothing is forgotten, from water bottles to your whistle.

2. Keep Instructions Clear and Brief:

Demonstrate each drill and use simple language. For example, say, "Keep the ball close to your feet like it's a dog on a leash."

Explain drills with demonstrations and concise steps.

Example: Show how to pass using the inside of the foot. Point or touch the part of the boot the kids will be using. Then, once you've demonstrated, let kids try in pairs. This way you can see if they've understood what you've told them or if you need to break the skill down even more.

Tip: Check for understanding by asking, "Who can show me what we're about to do?"

Additional Example: Use cones or markers to visually outline the drill setup. Then you can mention the cones as you are explaining the drill (ie "We will be starting behind the red cone and dribbling through the yellow cones").

Additional Tip: Break down complex drills into smaller parts and build gradually. This might mean initially doing a skill like "happy feet" while standing in the one spot ,starting very slowly. And then as they become more confident, they can move forward or backwards while still performing happy feet.

Tip: Use visual aids like a whiteboard for complex skills or drills.

3. Stay Flexible:

Be ready to adapt if a drill isn't working. Have backup games or exercises ready to go.

Example: If players are losing focus during a drill, switch to a quick game like "Simon Says" which doesn't require any setting up.

CONCLUSION

A well-planned training session is a blend of structure and spontaneity. By focusing on skill development, engagement, and adaptability, you can create an environment where young players thrive and develop a lifelong love for soccer.

6

FUNDAMENTAL SOCCER SKILLS

Topics covered in "FUNDAMENTAL SOCCER SKILLS"

1. **Teaching Skills: Dribbling, Passing, Change of Direction, Shooting, Control, and Juggling**
2. **Adapting Techniques for 5–10 Year Olds**
3. **Progressive Drills to Build Confidence**

Mastering fundamental soccer skills is crucial for young players, as it lays the foundation for their development and enjoyment of the game.

Here's how to teach dribbling, passing, shooting, control and more fundamental soccer skills in a fun, age-appropriate way.

1. Teaching Dribbling, Passing, Shooting and Control

1. Dribbling:

Dribbling is a skill that children can practice at home by themselves. Teach players the correct technique and encourage them to practice as much as they can. Show them how to use the inside, outside, and sole of their foot to control the ball.

Here are the main points that will lead to becoming a good dribbler.

1. Keep the Ball Close

- Use small, gentle touches with the inside and outside of your feet to move the ball forward.
- The ball should stay close enough so you can stop or change direction quickly. If the ball is too far from the body you can't protect it and the opposition can steal it. This is a key point that you should re-enforce with your kids. It's no use being the fastest dribbler if you can't control the ball or stop it when required.

2. Use the Correct Part of Your Foot

- **Inside of the foot (between your big toe and the arch of your foot):** For precise control when moving side to side.
- **Outside of the foot (when pointing your toes towards the ground, it is between your little toe and the top of your foot):** To push the ball forward and change direction.
- **Sole of the foot (the part of the foot under the ball of your foot):** To stop or drag the ball gently in any direction.

3. Look Up Regularly

- Tell your players to not just stare at the ball. Keep your head up ("look at the road") to see where you're going and watch out for teammates or opponents.
- I like to show them how the ball can be stolen off them if they constantly keep their heads down: Have the children dribble around but they must keep their eyes down and can't look up. Then you (the coach) are allowed to see if you can steal the ball off them. You will find that you are able to

kick or steal the ball away from most of the kids as they won't see you coming until the last moment. So next round, make it so they can look up as often as the want and try the same thing. This time the children should see you coming and they will be able to change direction or shield the ball to keep possession.

4. Control Your Speed

- Start slow to keep control of the ball. All skills should start off slowly when learning. It's always best to do it correctly slowly and then get faster once the basics of the skill have been mastered.
- When dribbling in open space, use longer touches (ie one touch of the ball for every couple of steps). But stay balanced so you can adjust direction quickly if needed.

5. Protect the Ball

- Use your body to shield the ball from opponents. I like to say to my kids "Chicken wings!" which means get your arms up so they are bent like a chickens wings and therefore an opposition player will find it hard to get close enough to steal the ball. Show them how by flapping you chicken wings a making chicken sounds as you dribble around and let one or two of the kids try to steal the ball from you – they'll love it!
- Dribble with the foot furthest from the defender to make it harder for them to steal it. For example, while dribbling along, if a defender is trying to win the ball from the right hand side, try and dribble with the left foot which will keep it further from them (and make sure to keep your right chicken wing up to keep them away!).

Practice Tip:

- Set up cones or objects as obstacles and practice weaving through them with both feet. Tell the kids dribbling can be done anytime, anywhere.
- Alternate between your left and right foot to develop skill with both.

Dribbling is all about **control, direction, and awareness**. Make sure to tell your kids that with practice, they'll get faster and more confident but to always start of slow to learn the skill!

Some fundamental skills children should work on to improve their touch, control and feel for the ball to help with dribbling and other soccer skills are:

- Sole Rolls
- Tick Tocks (aka Happy Feet)
- Drag Backs

Sole Rolls:

A **"sole roll"** is a simple soccer move used to control the ball and change its position by rolling it with the bottom (sole) of your foot. Here's how to do Sole Rolls!

1. **Step 1: Place your foot on the ball** - Gently rest the bottom of your foot on top of the ball. Make sure you're balanced on your standing leg.
2. **Step 2: Roll the ball** - Using light pressure, roll the ball to one side or forward. You can roll it left, right, or in the direction you want to move.
3. **Step 3: Follow the ball** - As the ball moves, quickly reposition your foot to continue rolling the ball.

The sole roll is great for:

- **Changing direction** when dribbling.

- **Shielding the ball** from an opponent.
- **Keeping control** in tight spaces.

Practice Tip:

- Start by rolling the ball back and forth with one foot, standing in the one place, then practice rolling it side-to-side in a straight line.
- Use a light touch to avoid losing control of the ball.
- It's a simple but effective move that's perfect for young players learning to control the ball! Encourage them to practice at home - they can even do it while sitting in a chair or on the couch.

Game: "Rolling Races"

- **Setup:** Create a straight course with cones or markers about 5–10 yards apart.

How to Play:

- Players use only **sole rolls** to move the ball from the starting cone to the finish line.
- They must keep the ball under control and stay within the course boundaries.
- If the ball goes out of bounds, they restart from the last cone passed.
- Once they reach the finish line, they can dribble back or tag the next player in a relay format.
- **Variation:** Add zig-zag cones or small obstacles for players to roll the ball around for more control practice.
- **Objective:** Improve ball control and confidence with the sole of the foot while having fun.

Happy Feet (also known as Tick Tocks):

"Happy Feet" is a simple soccer skill that helps players improve their quick footwork and ball control by rapidly tapping the ball back and forth between their feet. Here's how to do Happy Feet!

How to Do Happy Feet:

1. **Stand with the ball in between your feet** - Place the ball stationary on the ground between your feet.
2. **Lightly tap the ball with one foot** - Use the inside of your foot to tap the ball to the opposite foot.
3. **Switch feet quickly** - Use the inside of your other foot to tap the ball back. Keep the ball moving between your feet in a steady rhythm (tick-tock, tick-tock).
4. **Stay balanced** - Keep your knees slightly bent, stay light on your toes, and shift your weight as you move.

Key Tips:

- **Use soft touches** to keep the ball under control.
- **Keep your head up** as much as possible to develop awareness.
- **Start slow**, then gradually increase your speed as you get more comfortable.

Why It's Useful:

- Improves **foot speed** and **touch**.
- Helps with **coordination** and builds confidence in tight spaces.
- Teaches players to be comfortable using both feet.

Practice Challenge:

- Set a timer for 30 seconds and see how many taps you can do without losing control.
- Try adding movement by tapping the ball forward (or any direction) while

doing happy feet.

It's a fun and effective way for players to develop their touch and rhythm with the ball! And once again, children can perform this skill while sat at home on the couch.

Toe Taps:
Toe Taps are a simple skill that helps to develop foot coordination and balance by alternating taps on the top of the ball with the toes of each foot. Here's how to do Toe Taps!

1. Stand behind the ball with your knees slightly bent.
2. Lightly tap the top of the ball with the toes of one foot.
3. Quickly switch feet and tap the ball with the other foot.
4. Continue alternating taps in a steady rhythm.
5. Young children will struggle at first so make sure to go very slowly: tap the top of the ball with one foot, return that foot to the ground, then use the other foot to tap the top of the ball, return that foot to the ground and repeat.

- **Why Toe Taps are important:** Improves coordination, balance, and comfort with the ball.

Drill: "Toe Tap Station Challenge"
Setup: Place 5 cones in a straight line, about 3–5 steps apart.
How to Play: Players start at one end of the line, performing toe taps on the ball as they move forward.
When they reach a cone, they must circle around it while continuing toe taps.
Complete the course and then dribble back to the start.
Variation: Time the players to see how fast they can complete the challenge while keeping control of the ball.
Objective: Improve balance and control while adding a movement compo-

nent.

Pull-Backs:

Pull-Backs are a move to stop the ball and quickly change direction by pulling it backward with the sole of the foot.

Here's how to do Pull-Backs!

1. Place your foot on top of the ball.
2. Roll the ball backward slightly while stepping back with your other foot.
3. Turn your body to follow the ball and continue dribbling.

- **Why it's important:** Teaches players how to maintain control and escape from tight situations. Where'd he go??

(These skills plus more games and coaching kids advice are in "Coaching Kids Soccer Volume 2" book which is available on Amazon).

Game: "Escape the Defender"

Setup: Create a 10x10-yard grid with cones. Designate one player as the defender.

How to Play:

Players dribble their ball around the grid while the defender moves to tag them (no ball for the defender).

If the defender gets close, the dribbling player performs a pull-back to change direction and escape. If a defender performs a pull back they cannot be tagged.

If tagged, players complete a fun task like 5 jumping jacks or 5 toe taps before rejoining the game.

Variation: Add more defenders for advanced players.

Objective: Teach kids to use pull-backs in real game situations to avoid pressure from defenders.

Inside-Outside Dribble:

The Inside-Outide Dribble is a basic dribbling move to change direction using the inside and outside of your foot.

Here's how to do it!
1. Push the ball slightly to the side with the inside of your foot.
2. Quickly use the outside of the same foot to tap the ball in the opposite direction.
3. Repeat with the other foot.

- **Why it's important:** Helps with quick direction changes and builds control with both sides of the foot.

Drill: "Zig-Zag Cone Dribble"

Setup: Set up a zig-zag course using cones spaced 3–5 steps apart.
How to Play:
Players dribble through the cones, alternating inside and outside touches with the same foot.

After completing the course, players dribble back using the other foot.

Focus on keeping the ball close and controlled while weaving through the cones.

Variation: Add a time challenge to increase difficulty.
Objective: Improve dribbling control and quick changes of direction.

Dribbling Drills:

- **Example 1:** Start with simple dribbling exercises, such as moving the ball in straight lines using the inside of their foot.
- Tip: Remind them to keep their head up and "look at the road" as often as they can while dribbling to avoid collisions.
- Encourage close ball control by having players dribble within small areas.

- **Game Idea:** "Cone Snakes," where players weave through cones placed close together like a snake, pretending they are escaping a jungle.
- Tip: Use creative prompts like "pretend the ball is your pet and keep it close so it doesn't run away."

- **Example 2**: Create a "Dribble and Stop" game where players dribble and freeze on your whistle. Make sure they have the ball close enough that they can stop when they hear your whistle. Players get a point each time they can stop their ball within one second of the whistle. Note: This game is also called **"Traffic Lights"** or **"Red Light/Green Light"**
- Tip: Add variations, like dribbling only with the left foot, to build non-dominant foot confidence.

2. Passing:

Focus on accuracy by teaching players to pass the ball with the inside of their foot (where the Nike swoosh or Adidas 3 stripes are on the inside of a soccer boot). Remember to demonstrate first. I always like to tap the part of the boot with my hand that they should be using to pass the ball.

When first learning to pass, teach the players to plant their non-passing foot next to the ball pointing in the direction they want the ball to go. Then swing their passing leg back from the hip like a pendulum and strike the ball with the inside of the foot, following through towards their target.

Make sure to lock the ankle when striking the ball to keep it strong like their favourite super hero!

Start with passes over a very short distance, increasing the distance as they become more confident and accurate.

Drill Example: "Target Passing," where players aim for a player, a cone or small goal 5-10 yards away.

Tip: Challenge them to pass using both their dominant and non-dominant foot for versatility.

Introduce teamwork with pair or group passing drills.

Game Idea: "Pass and Move," where players must pass and then run to a new cone to receive the next pass, mimicking game scenarios.

Tip 1: Praise good technique and encourage players to communicate by saying "I'm open!" or "Here!"

Tip 2: Gradually increase the passing distance to challenge control and accuracy.

Game Idea 2: "Gates". Set up an area with pairs of cones spread around. Pair the players up with one ball for each pair. Players must then move around the area, passing the ball to each other through the gates. How many gates can they pass through in a set amount of time? Note: Players must not go back through the same gate they just passed through.

Note: Receiving the ball with good control is just as important as being a good passer of the ball! Make sure to show players how to cushion the ball when receiving the pass so it doesn't just hit their foot and end up 5 yards away for an opposition player to steal. Players should bring their foot (or thigh or chest) back with the ball as it makes contact with them so as to cushion and absorb the impact.

3. Change of Direction:

It's great to be able to dribble fast in a straight line. But children also need to be able to change direction to get out of trouble! Introduce simple moves like the "drag back" or "inside cut" to help kids change direction while dribbling.

- **Example 1:** Set up cones as defenders and have players practice turning, dragging, or cutting away from them. I find that using cones as defenders when first learning a skill builds confidence. There isn't pressure from a defender so players can learn at their own pace. Let them make mistakes and tell them that is part of learning a new skill.
- Tip: Use visual cues like holding up a brightly coloured cone or bib to signify a direction changes during a dribbling drill. This helps players look at their surroundings.

- **Example 2:** Create a "Turn-and-Go" drill where players dribble, turn at a cone, and accelerate.
- Tip: Encourage kids to use their non-dominant foot to turn.

- **Example 3:** Introduce "Zig-Zag Dribbling," where players weave through a staggered cone layout. This helps with changing direction.
- Tip: Challenge them to perform a specific turn (like a drag back) at each

cone.

4. Shooting:

Shoot! yells the crowd. It's easy from the sidelines isn't it? But to become an accurate striker takes time and practice - and good technique. When you strike a ball, sometimes you forgo accuracy for power. Passing is easier because there usually isn't as much force compared to shooting.

- **Teach the basics:** Step up to the ball and plant the non-kicking foot next to the ball. Lock the ankle of the kicking foot, use the laces area to strike the ball and follow through with the strike. Once again, demonstrate and touch the part of the boot with your hand that you want the kids to strike the ball with. This always helps them to picture in their head what they should be doing.

- Tip 1: Make sure the players don't lean back while striking the ball. Encourage them to have their shoulders over the ball as they make contact
- Tip 2: And remind them to glance at the goal before shooting so they can "pick their spot".
- Once they are more advanced, encourage power and accuracy by aiming at marked areas of the goal (place a cone or a pole inside the goals for the kids to aim at. Or hang a bib off the cross bar if you want them to go for the top corners).

Game Idea 1: "Hit the Corners"
How to Play:

- Players score extra points for hitting top or bottom corners. Place cones for them to aim at or bibs as mentioned above.

- 1 point for a regular goal or 3 points for hitting a cone or bib. Or maybe the coach has to do 5 push ups every time the kids hit a cone?

Game Idea 2: "Shoot Past the Monster"

Setup: Set up a goal. Add a "monster" (the coach or a parent) in front of the goal who moves side to side pretending to guard the goal.

How to Play:

- Line the kids up a few meters away from the goal with a ball each.
- The aim is to "shoot" past the monster into the goal. **If they score a certain amount of goals, they "defeat" the monster.**
- Kids can all be shooting at once or take it in turns (as long as there isn't a long line – we don't want kids getting bored and not being involved).
- The monster can playfully act dramatic when hit by a ball, or angry when a goal is scored or pretend to be tricky by moving around.
- **Why It Works:** This game makes shooting practice exciting and builds accuracy and confidence. It also encourages kids to think about timing and placement when shooting as they must avoid the monster.
- **Pro tip:** To keep count of the score during a game or shooting contest like this, have a stack of cones on the side of the pitch or beside the goal. Then each time a goal is scored, the child can run and grab a cone and place it down so it is clear what the score is. The children love being the one that scores and gets to put a cone out!

Game Idea 3: "Stop the Zombie"

Setup:

- The coach (or parent) acts as the "zombie" guarding a goal or target area.
- Place 3 cones in front of the goal to represent obstacles the kids must dribble through before shooting.
- Place one different coloured cone 5 or 10 yards in front of the goal.

How to Play:

- Each player must dribble through the 3 cones to get close enough to the goal and shoot to "stop the zombie."
- The zombie is staggering out from goal, trying to reach the different coloured cone.
- Each time a goal is scored the zombie is stunned and must stumble back a couple steps.
- When the zombie reaches the cone they are free to chase the children, pretending to eat them! Watch the children run and listen to them squeal!

Why It Works: It adds excitement and movement to shooting practice, combining dribbling, accuracy, and fun storytelling. Kids love the thrill of "escaping" the zombie!

5. Control:

Teach children to trap the ball with their foot, thigh, or chest, depending on the pass.

- **Drill Example:** "First Touch Challenge," where players control a gently tossed ball and pass it back. This can be done in pairs with one player being the server for a minute (or 10-15 throws) and then swap roles.
- Tip: Use a variety of passes—rolling, bouncing, or lofted—to develop adaptability.
- Encourage soft touches (cushioning) to keep the ball close and ready for the next move. Tell them to pretend the ball is an egg and they should move the part of their body they are controlling the ball with back with the ball so as to cushion the egg (ball) and not break it!

Basic Soccer Game to help with ball control:

Game 1 "Body Ball":

Purpose: Teach young kids how to control the ball using different parts of their body (feet, thighs, chest, etc.) in a fun and engaging way.

Setup:

1. Mark a small playing area (10x10 yards works well).
2. Give each player a soccer ball.

How to Play:

1. Players start dribbling their ball slowly within the marked area.
2. The coach (or parent) calls out a body part, such as:

- **"Foot!"** – Players must stop the ball with their foot.
- **"Thigh!"** – Players pick up the ball, toss it up, and trap it with their thigh.
- **"Chest!"** – Players pick up the ball, toss it up, and control it with their chest.
- **"Head!"** – Players gently head the ball after tossing it up.

Players must perform the action as quickly as possible while staying in control of their ball.

Key Focus Points:

- **Control:** Encourage gentle, controlled touches to prevent the ball from bouncing away.
- **Balance:** Teach kids to stay balanced when using different body parts.
- **Engagement:** Keep the pace lively by alternating body parts quickly.

Game 2 " "Control Island"
Setup:

- Set up several small "islands" using cones (these can be 5x5 yards for each player or have larger islands where there can be a few players. Each island represents the area where the players must control their ball.
- Have the coach or a helper serve balls from a central area.

How to Play:

1. The kids start on their islands. The coach throws or rolls balls toward the islands, and the kids must control the ball and keep it on their island. 1.

- **Feet Control:** Stop the ball with the inside or sole of the foot and keep it on the island.
- **Thigh Control:** Use the thigh to cushion the ball, letting it drop to the ground gently.
- **Chest Control:** Use the chest by leaning back with the ball to stop it and keep it on the island.

2. After controlling the ball, the kids can dribble it back to the coach to return it and prepare for another turn.

Variations:

- Shrink the islands to challenge the children to have even closer control.
- Pretend their is ocean all around and they must keep their ball safe from falling in the shark infested waters.

Why It Works:
This game combines fun, imagination, and practical control skills. It helps kids focus on accuracy and soft touches while adding a challenge to keep their attention.

Game 3: "Popcorn Control"

Setup:

- Create a large circle using cones and have all the kids stand inside with one or two coaches outside the circle.
- The coach has several soccer balls and acts as the "popcorn popper." Grab a parent to help with this one so more balls can be served.

How to Play:

1. The coach tosses or rolls balls randomly into the circle, calling out the part of the body the kids should use to control the ball (e.g., feet, thigh, chest).

2. The kids must quickly move to the nearest ball and control it using the specified body part.

- **Feet:** Trap or stop the ball softly.
- **Thigh:** Cushion it so it drops to the ground gently.
- **Chest:** Absorb the impact and guide the ball downward.

3. After controlling the ball, the kids push it out of the circle and get ready for the next "popcorn."

Variations:

- Increase the speed of the game to challenge reaction times.
- Add a time limit to see how many balls the group can control collectively.

Why It Works:

This game keeps kids moving and reacting quickly, building their coordination and control skills in an engaging way. The randomness makes it unpredictable and fun!

6. Juggling:

Juggling helps kids develop coordination, touch, and control over the ball. Start with simple steps to build their confidence.

Basic Steps to Teach Juggling:

1. Start Small:

- Have kids hold the ball with their hands and drop it onto their dominant foot (remember to demonstrate and show them what part of their foot or body they are using).
- Kick the ball back up and catch it with their hands. Repeat several times.

2. Add One Touch:

- Once they're comfortable, encourage them to kick the ball up twice in a row before catching it.
- Gradually add more touches as they improve.

3. Use Both Feet:

- Alternate between the right and left foot to develop balance and coordination.

4. Introduce Other Body Parts:

- Teach them to control the ball with their thighs, chest and eventually their head.

5. Stay Relaxed:

- Encourage kids to focus on light, controlled touches and keep the ball close to their body.

Game 1: "Juggling Ladder"
Purpose: Build juggling confidence and reward progress.

Setup:

1. Create a "ladder" using cones or markers, with each cone representing a juggling goal (e.g., 1 juggle, 2 juggles, 3 juggles, etc.).
2. Each child has a soccer ball.

How to Play:

1. Players start at the first cone and attempt to juggle the ball once before catching it.
2. If successful, they move to the next cone and attempt two juggles, then three, and so on.
3. If they fail, they stay at their current cone and try again until they succeed.
4. The goal is to advance through the ladder, increasing the number of consecutive juggles at each step.

Variations:

1. **Timed Challenge:** See how far players can climb the ladder in 5 minutes.
2. **Partner Play:** Pair kids up, and they take turns juggling and cheering each other on.
3. **Body Part Challenge:** Add specific tasks, like juggling with only the thigh or alternating feet.

Why It Works:

- Breaks juggling into achievable steps, building confidence gradually.

- Keeps practice fun and competitive.
- Encourages kids to set personal goals and celebrate progress.

2. Adapting Techniques for 5-10 Year Olds

Here are some techniques to help you get the most out of coaching young children.

1. Keep It Simple:

Focus on one aspect of a skill at a time. For instance, when teaching dribbling, start with inside-foot control before introducing other techniques.

Example: Break down dribbling into "push the ball," "chase the ball," and "stop the ball."

Tip: Use cones or lines as visual guides to help players stay on track.

2. Use Age-Appropriate Language:

Replace technical terms with fun and relatable descriptions.

Example: Instead of "ankle locked," say "make your foot strong like a superhero."

Tip: Turn instructions into mini-stories to keep kids engaged, like "your foot is the superhero shielding and protecting the ball."

3. Encourage Creativity:

Let kids experiment with different moves and techniques during drills.

Game Idea: "Trick Shot Time," where players invent and showcase their unique ways of scoring.

Tip: Encourage them to name their moves, such as "The Tornado Spin," to build ownership and confidence.

4. Adjust Equipment and Space:

Use smaller fields and lighter balls to match the kids' size and strength.

Example: For younger players, use size 3 balls and reduce the size of the playing area to encourage more touches.

Tip: Create mini-challenges within the space, like "can you dribble from one goal to the other in 10 seconds?"

3. Progressive Drills to Build Confidence

1. Start Simple:

Begin with static drills to introduce a skill in a controlled environment.

Example: "Stationary Passing," where players practice passing to a partner without moving.

Tip: Focus on body positioning and foot placement to build strong fundamentals.

2. Add Movement:

Progress to dynamic drills that incorporate running or game-like scenarios.

Example: "Pass and Chase," where players pass the ball and then run to follow it.

Tip: Encourage players to call out "pass", "go" or "I'm free" to practice communication.

3. Introduce Defenders:

Build confidence by adding light pressure from defenders as players improve.

Example: "1v1 Challenges," where players dribble past a defender to score in a small goal.

Tip: Teach defenders to use shadowing techniques instead of going directly for the ball to maintain fairness. This means putting pressure on the player but not actually trying to kick or win the ball.

4. Combine Skills:

Create drills that combine multiple skills, such as dribbling i a pass or trapping into a shot.

Example: "Control and Shoot," where players control a pass, dribble briefly, and then shoot at goal.

Game Idea: "Skill Relay," where players complete a sequence of dribbling, passing, and shooting before tagging the next teammate.

Tip: Add timers to the relay to create friendly competition.

5. Use Games to Reinforce Learning:

Incorporate small-sided games that encourage players to use their newly developed skills.

Example: "Five-Pass Challenge," where teams earn points for completing five consecutive passes during play.

Tip: Reward effort and teamwork rather than focusing solely on winning.

CONCLUSION

By focusing on the fundamentals and adapting techniques to suit the developmental stages of 5–10-year-olds, you can help young players build skills, confidence, and a love for the game. Always celebrate their progress, no matter how small, and make learning soccer a joyful experience.

> **Enjoying this book so far?** *If you're finding these coaching tips helpful, I would greatly appreciate it if you could leave an honest review on Amazon. Simply head to the book on Amazon*
> **USA REVIEW LINK:** *https://www.Amazon.com/review*
> **UK REVIEW LINK:** *https://www.Amazon.co.uk/review/create-review?&asin=B0D48YQ1DH*

and scroll down 'til you see "Write A Customer Review" tab on the left. Your feedback helps other parents and volunteers discover this resource and join the journey of positive coaching!

7

BEYOND THE BALL: DEVELOPING PERCEPTION AND DECISION MAKING IN YOUNG SOCCER PLAYERS

Topics covered in "BEYOND THE BALL: DEVELOPING PERCEPTION AND DECISION MAKING IN YOUNG SOCCER PLAYERS"

1. **Why Perception and Decision Making Matter**
2. **Developing Perception: "Eyes Up, Head Up!"**
3. **Decision-Making: Choosing the Best Play**
4. **Bringing It All Together: Seeing, Thinking, Acting**
5. **Making It Fun & Letting Them Learn**

We all know dribbling, passing, and shooting are key parts of soccer. They're the tools players use to make things happen on the field. But what if a player doesn't know when or where to use them?

That's where **perception and decision-making** come in. These skills help young players see, think and play smarter. These are the often-overlooked skills that turn a technically decent player into a **smart** one. This chapter is all about helping young players (ages 5-10) learn to **scan the field, make quick decisions, and play with confidence.**

Why Perception and Decision Making Matter

Imagine a player who can dribble like Messi... but only looks down at the ball. They might weave through cones like a pro, but in a game, they'll miss open teammates, run straight into defenders, and waste good chances.

Perception is about **seeing the game**—not just the ball at their feet. It means scanning for teammates, defenders, and space. Once a player sees what's happening, they can make a decision:

- Should I **dribble** or **pass**?
- If I pass, **to whom**?
- Should I **shoot** now or take another touch?

Perception and decision-making go hand in hand. A great pass is useless if it's to a teammate under pressure. Likewise, a perfect decision to pass means nothing if the execution is sloppy.

So, how do we help kids **see the game better** and make **smarter choices**? Let's dive into some practical ways to train these skills!

Developing Perception: "Eyes Up, Head Up!"

Young players tend to focus only on the ball. Our job as coaches is to **expand their vision** so they can take in everything happening around them. Think of it like learning to drive—at first, you focus only on the steering wheel, but with experience, you start scanning the road, checking mirrors, and reacting to traffic all at once.

Here are some **fun drills** to help kids **see the game better:**

1. "Colour Call-Out"

Goal: Train players to keep their heads up while dribbling.

How to play:

- Players dribble inside a marked area.
- The coach holds up a coloured cone or bib.
- Players must **call out the colour** while dribbling. Bonus point to the first two players to call out the colour/s.

Progression:

- Increase dribbling speed.
- Use multiple colours and ask players to call out two at a time.

Coaching Tip: "Glance up quickly, then back down to control the ball—just like checking your mirrors while driving!"

2. "Find the Open Teammate"

Goal: Improve awareness of teammates.

How to play:

- Players dribble inside a grid.
- The coach calls out two teammate's name.
- The players must **find each other and pass** while still moving.

Progression:

- Add defenders to make it harder.
- Give a time limit for passing.

Coaching Tip: "See before you pass—don't just kick and hope!"

Decision-Making: Choosing the Best Play

Once players can **see** what's happening, they need to decide **what to do next.** This is where we encourage kids to think about options instead of just reacting.

Here are some **small-sided games** that **force quick decisions:**

1. **"Two-Touch Soccer"**

Goal: Develop quick thinking and passing under pressure.
How to play:

- Players can only **take two touches** before passing or shooting.
- If they take more, the other team gets the ball.

Progression:

- Allow **one free touch per play** to allow for learning.
- Play in **smaller areas** to increase speed of play.

Coaching Tip: "Think before the ball comes—your next move starts in your head!"

2. **"Pass or Dribble?"**

Goal: Help players decide when to pass and when to take defenders on.
How to play:

- Two players with one ball dribble toward a defender.

- The player with the ball must **decide whether to pass to their teammate or take the defender on 1v1**.
- If they get past, they **shoot on goal.**

Progression:

- Add a second defender for more decision-making pressure.

Coaching Tip: "Read the defender—if they're backing off, attack! If they're closing fast, pass!"

Bringing It All Together: Seeing, Thinking, Acting

These drills help players **connect the dots** between **seeing** the field, **thinking** about the best option, and **acting** on it. Here are some **coaching cues** to reinforce these ideas:

Perception Cues:

- "Look up before you pass!"
- "Scan like a GPS—where's the space?"
- "Who's open? Who's really open?"

Decision-Making Cues:

- "Pass or dribble—what's the better choice?"
- "Is your teammate in a good position?"
- "Think quick, but don't rush!"

By repeating these phrases in training and games, kids will start making better decisions instinctively.

Making It Fun & Letting Them Learn

At the end of the day, soccer is about **playing, exploring, and making mistakes.** The best way to help young players develop perception and decision-making is to **let them play** and figure things out naturally.

Here's how to **keep it fun and effective:**

- **Use small-sided games**—more action, more decisions, more learning.
- **Encourage creativity**—don't over-coach; let them experiment.
- **Praise effort, not just results**—reward players for trying to look up and think ahead.
- **Make it competitive**—challenges like "who can make the smartest pass?" keep kids engaged.

CONCLUSION

Helping young players **see the field, think quickly, and make smart choices** is just as important as teaching them how to pass or shoot.

By mixing **fun drills, small-sided games, and simple coaching cues,** you'll set your players up to be more confident, aware, and effective on the field. They won't just be kicking a ball—they'll be **thinking, reacting, and playing smarter.**

And who knows? Maybe the next time they step on the field, you'll see a **pass, dribble, or shot that makes you think... "Yep, they're getting it!"**

Now that's coaching done right!

8

EIGHT TRAINING SESSION PLANS

Topics covered in "EIGHT TRAINING SESSION PLANS"

1. **Training Session Plan 1: Passing**
2. **Training Session Plan 2: Dribbling**
3. **Training Session Plan 3: Shooting**
4. **Training Session Plan 4: 1v1 Play**
5. **Training Session Plan 5: Passing**
6. **Training Session Plan 6: Dribbling**
7. **Training Session Plan 7: Shooting**
8. **Training Session Plan 8: 1v1 Play**

We touched on how to plan and run a training session in the first chapter. But in this chapter I've done the work for you and come up with eight fun training sessions for young players. If you train your team once a week you've got eight weeks worth of training sessions ready to go!

If these sessions aren't enough for you, grab my other kids soccer book "Coaching Kids Soccer Volumes 1,2,3" which has loads more games, all with diagrams, descriptions and coaching points!

These sessions below cover the four main soccer fundamentals:

1. **Passing**
2. **Dribbling**
3. **Shooting**
4. **1v1 Play**

Each session focusses on one of these fundamentals (ie the first session is on passing, the second session is on dribbling, etc).

They are based on my soccer training session template below that breaks a training session into 5 parts. If you have an hour session you can run each of the 5 parts for 10 minutes, which allows 10 spare minutes for setting up of drills, instructions and water breaks.

The 5 parts are:

1. SMALL SIDED GAME
2. FUN SOCCER GAME
3. *SMALL SIDED GAME (*with a focus on encouraging the main skill of the session)
4. FUN SOCCER GAME
5. SMALL SIDED GAME

EIGHT TRAINING SESSION PLANS

TRAINING SESSION PLAN   DATE

FOCUS OF SESSION

1 SMALL SIDED GAME

2 FUN SOCCER GAME

3 SMALL SIDED GAME

ENCOURAGE SKILL BEING WORKED ON
(IE PASSING, DRIBBLING, SHOOTING, 1v1)

4 FUN SOCCER GAME

5 SMALL SIDED GAME

I like to start all my session off with a small sided game! This way the kids can get straight into it, burn off some excess energy and then they are keen to come to training next time because they know they'll play a game straight away.

If you have a team with all first time players, that haven't played soccer before or developed many basic skills, I would suggest swapping out one of the 10 minute small sided games for working on a particular skill so they can improve.

Training Session Plan 1: Passing

1. Small-Sided Game (10 minutes)

Set up a 20x15 meter field for 4v4 or 5v5 games. Encourage kids to pass to teammates instead of dribbling.

2. Fun Soccer Game: "Through the Gate" (10 minutes)

EIGHT TRAINING SESSION PLANS

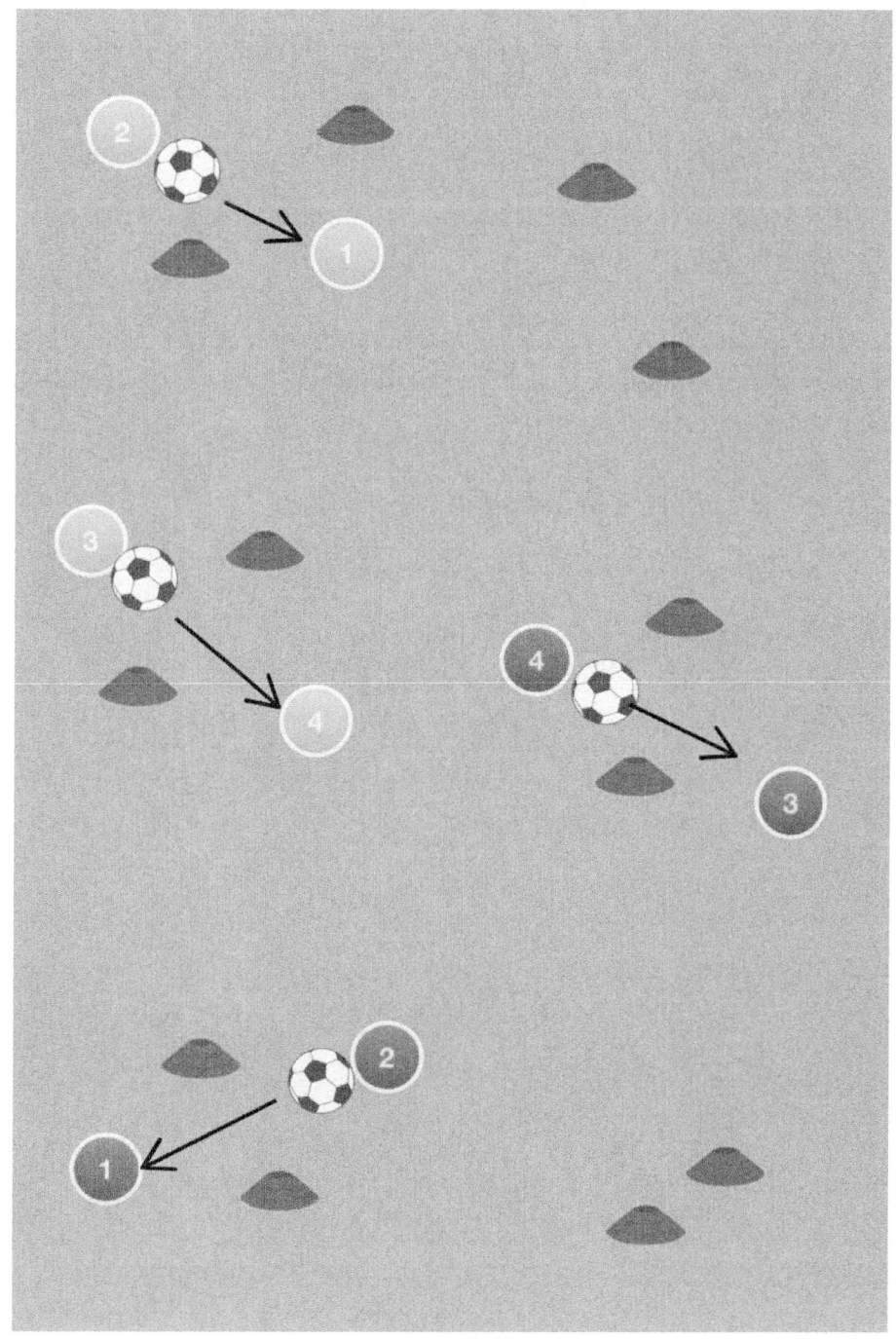

- **Setup:** Mark out several pairs of cones (gates) in a 20x20 yard grid.
- **Activity:** Players pair up and pass the ball back and forth through the gates, counting how many they can complete in a minute. They cannot go back through the same gate until they have passed through a different one.
- **Progression:** Make gates smaller or introduce defenders (or the coach) to apply light pressure.

3. Small-Sided Game Emphasising Passing (10 minutes)

Play another small-sided game, but award an extra point for goals scored after three consecutive passes.

4. Fun Soccer Game: "Knock the Ball" (10 minutes)

EIGHT TRAINING SESSION PLANS

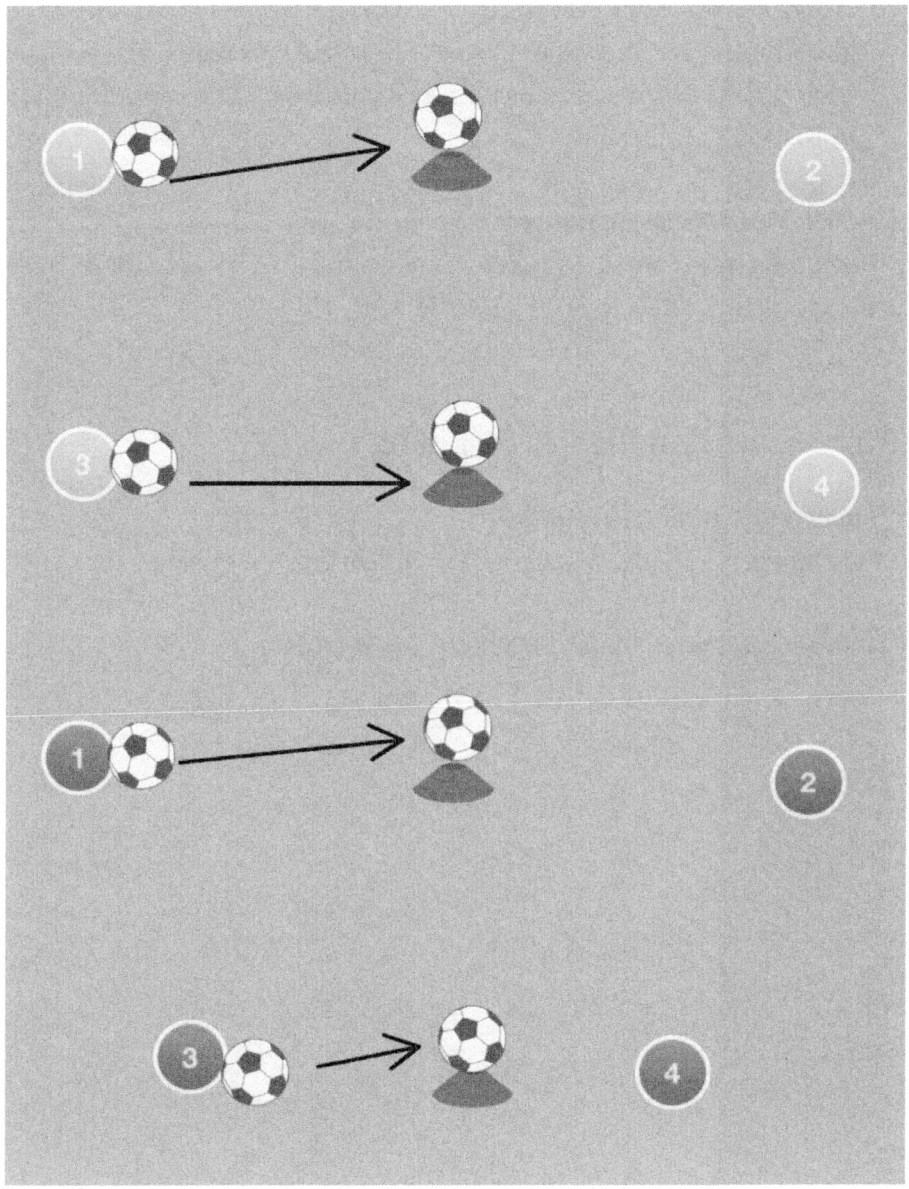

- **Setup:** Place soccer balls on top of cones.
- **Activity:** Players pair up and go opposite sides of the cone and attempt to knock the balls off the cones by passing. Replace the ball each time it

is knocked off. Adjust distances based on skill level. (Note: Notice the bottom pair (dark 3 & 4) are closer to the cone. These two players may have only just started playing soccer so you can make it easier for them by reducing the distance).

5. Small-Sided Game (10 minutes)

End with a free-play small-sided game, focusing on fun and letting kids apply the passing skills they've practised.

Training Session Plan 2: Dribbling

1. Small-Sided Game (10 minutes)

Let players start with a 4v4 game. Encourage them to dribble

2. Fun Soccer Game: "Gates Dribbling" (10 minutes)

EIGHT TRAINING SESSION PLANS

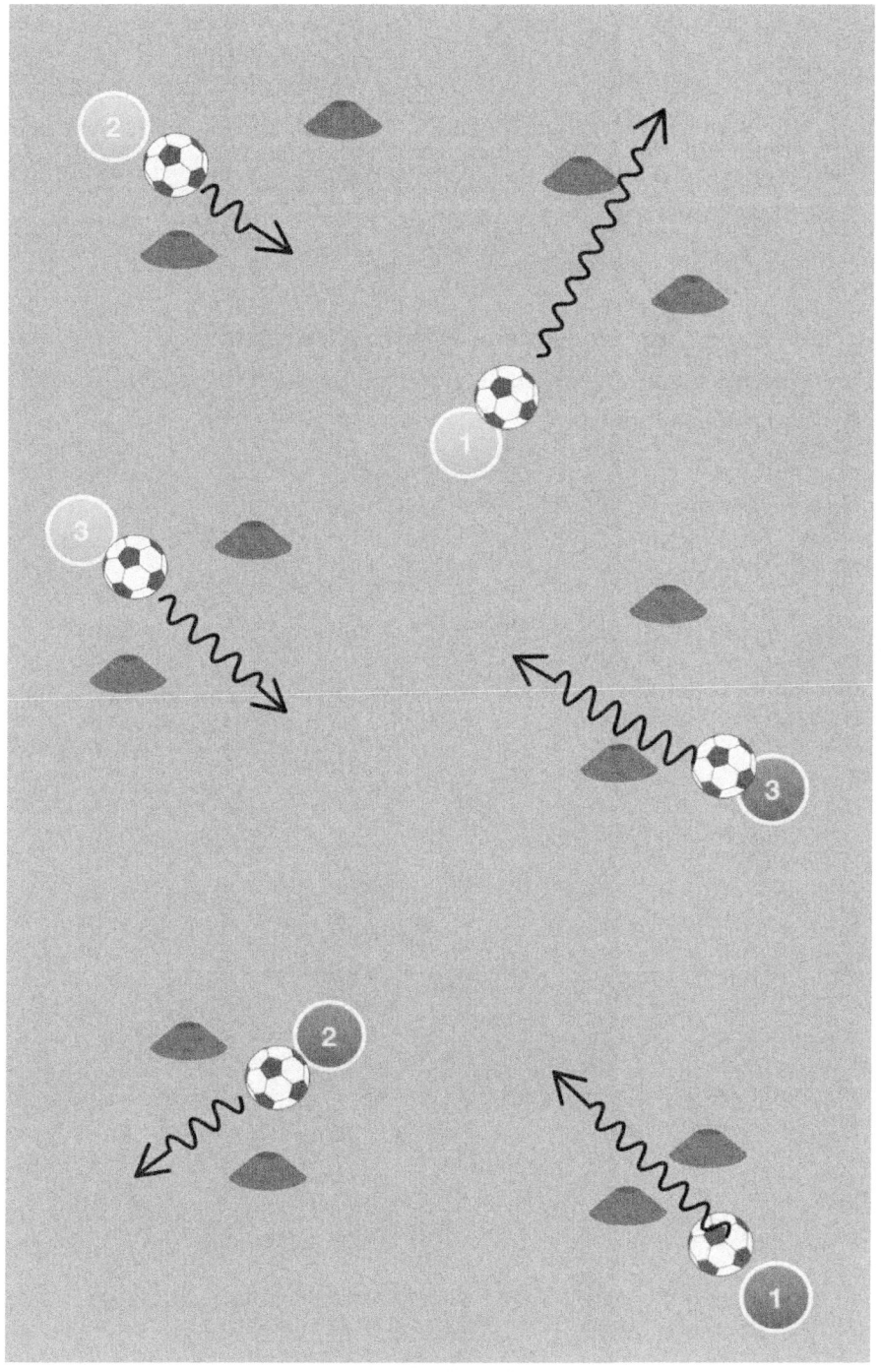

- **Setup:** Scatter several pairs of cones (gates) across the field.
- **Activity:** Players dribble through as many gates as possible in one minute, avoiding collisions.
- **Progression:** Add defenders or make gates smaller for advanced players.

3. Small-Sided Game Emphasising Dribbling (10 minutes)

Play another game but reward players an extra point for goals scored after a dribble past an opponent.

4. Fun Soccer Game: "Traffic Lights" (10 minutes)

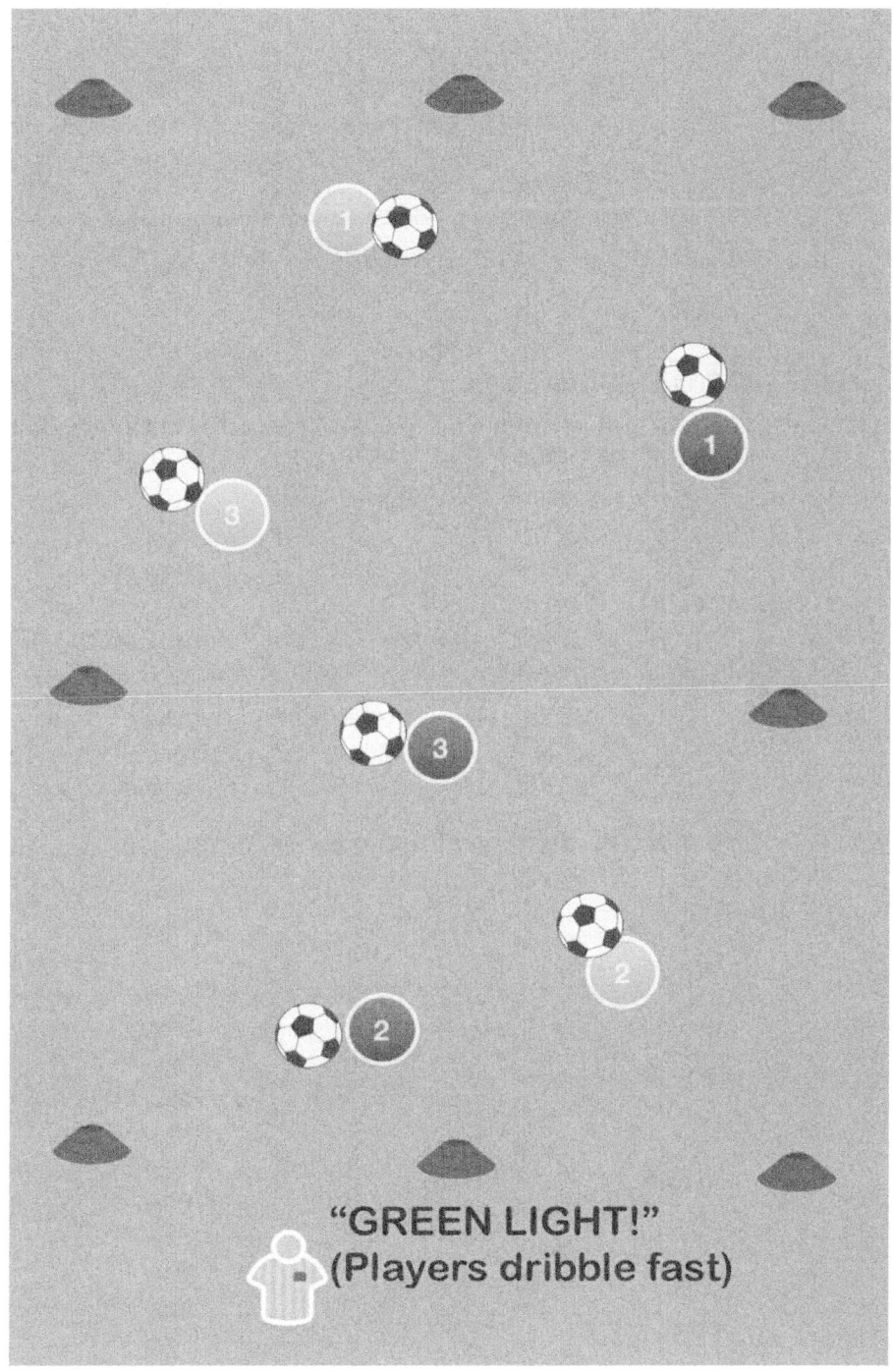

- **Setup:** Players dribble inside a marked area.
- **Activity:** Call out "Green Light" (dribble fast), "Yellow Light" (slow dribble), and "Red Light" (stop ball). Add other commands, like "Reverse" (dribble backward). You can give the kids a cone to use as a pretend steering wheel.

5. Small-Sided Game (10 minutes)

End with a fun small-sided game where kids can apply their dribbling skills freely.

Training Session Plan 3: Shooting

1. Small-Sided Game (10 minutes)

Play a 4v4 game, encouraging players to take shots whenever they have space. Praise attempts, even if they miss.

2. Fun Soccer Game: "Hit the Target" (10 minutes)

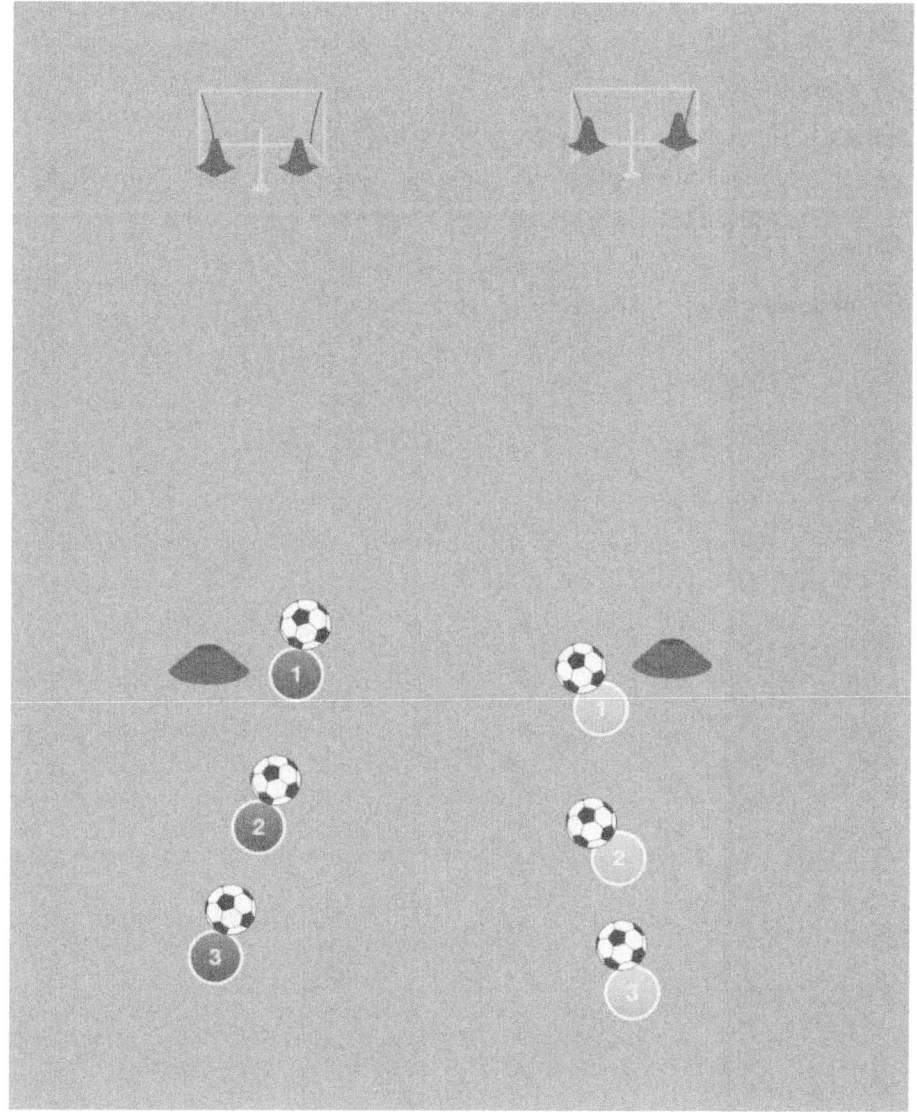

- **Setup:** Place different-sized targets (cones, poles, hoops, or hanging bibs) in various areas of the goal. Assign each target a point value based on difficulty (e.g., bottom corners = 1 point, top corners = 3 points).
- **Activity:** Players take turns shooting at the goal, trying to hit specific

targets. Call out a target before each shot to challenge accuracy. Keep score and see who can earn the most points in a set number of attempts.

3. Small-Sided Game Emphasising Shooting (10 minutes)

In this game, reward players for taking more shots. Add a rule where a high-five is given for every shot attempt, whether it scores or not.

4. Fun Soccer Game: "It's a Race" (10 minutes)

EIGHT TRAINING SESSION PLANS

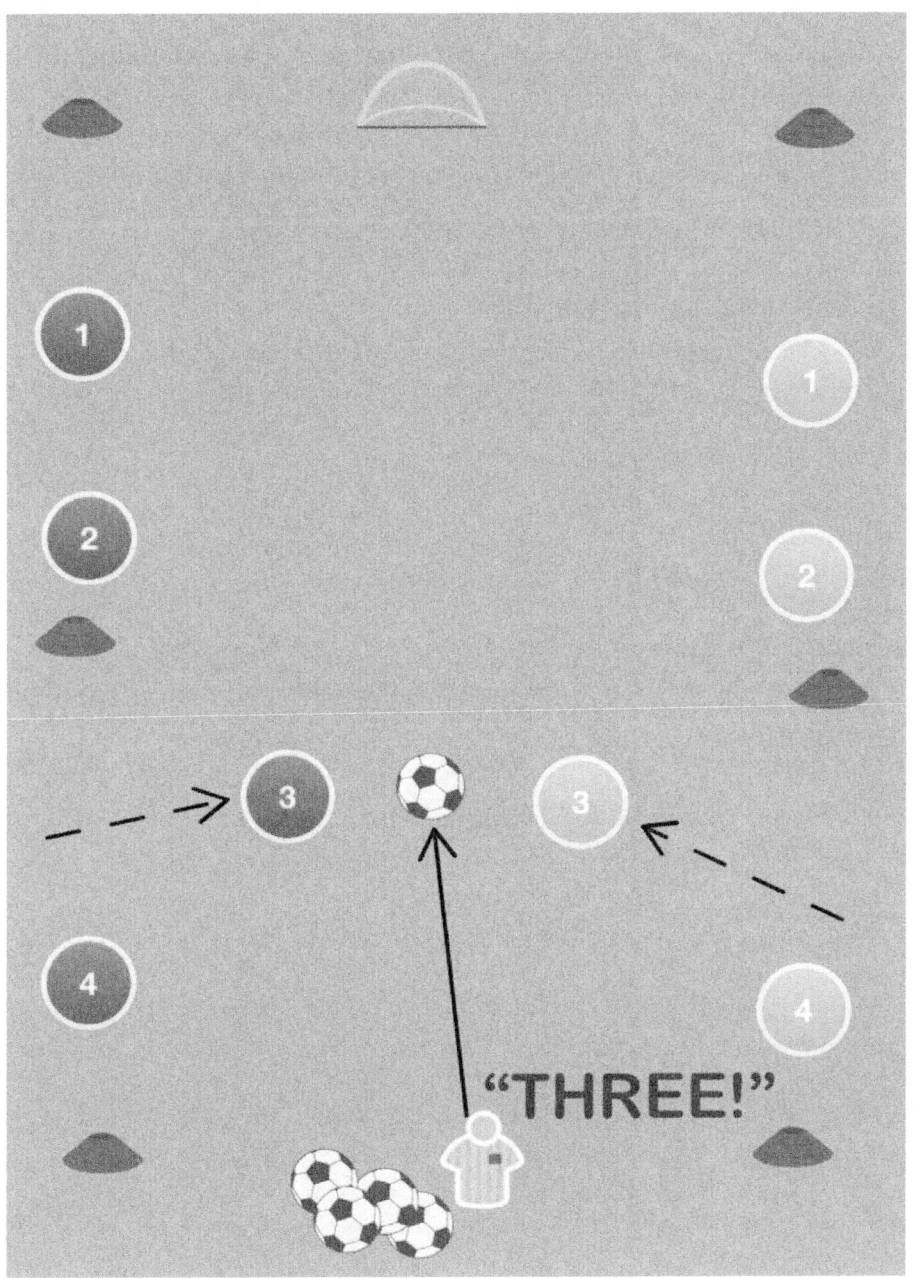

- **Setup:** Divide players into two teams, numbering them off and lining up opposite each other with balls in the centre (or the coach rolling them out).
- **Activity:** When you call out a number, those players race to the ball. The first player to the ball dribbles and takes a shot on goal while the other player defends.

5. Small-Sided Game (10 minutes)

End with a small-sided game, encouraging frequent shooting and applauding creativity.

Training Session Plan 4: 1v1 Play

1. Small-Sided Game (10 minutes)

Play a regular 4v4 game, focusing on encouraging players to take on opponents 1v1.

2. Fun Soccer Game: "King of the Ring" (10 minutes)

EIGHT TRAINING SESSION PLANS

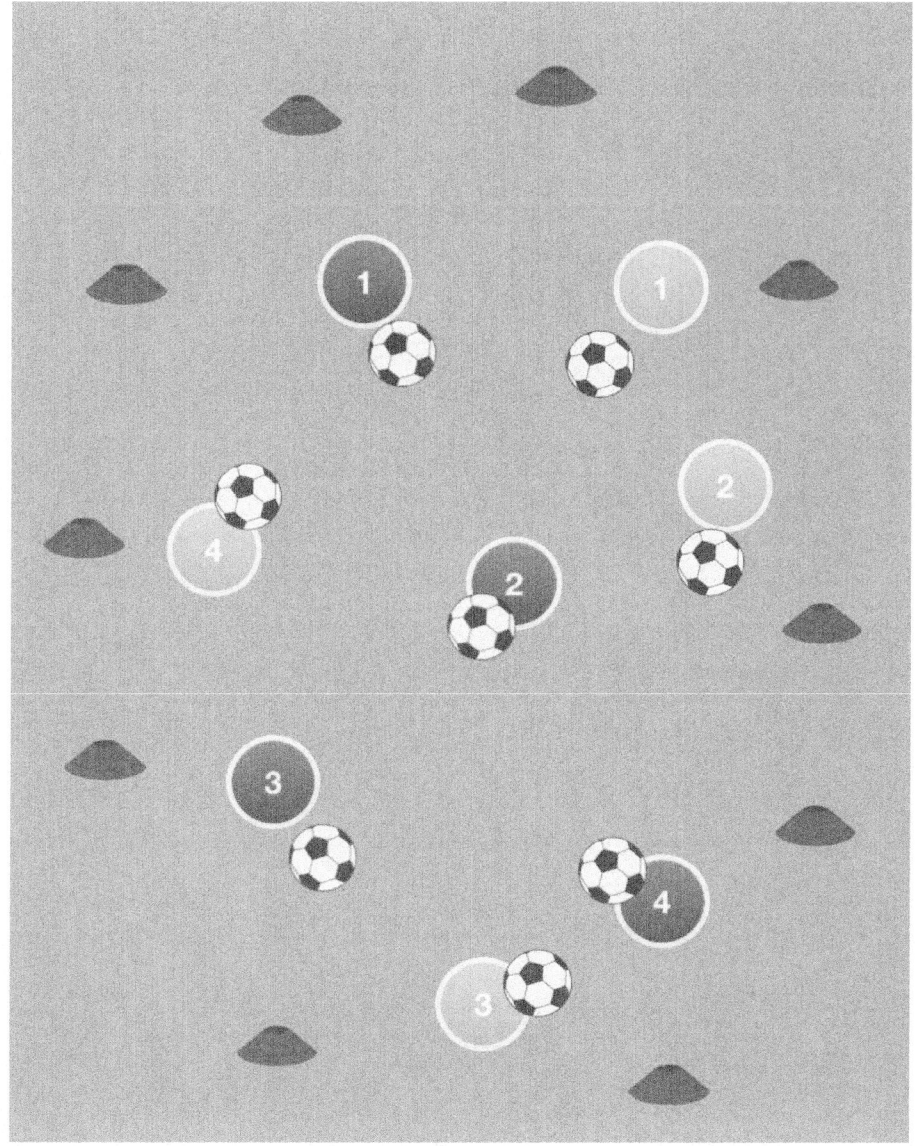

- **Setup:** Each player has a ball inside a defined area.
- **Activity:** Players try to keep possession of their ball while kicking others' balls out of the area. If a players ball is kicked out they must do 10 toe

taps and can then return.

3. Small-Sided Game Emphasising 1v1s (10 minutes)

Reward teams for players who successfully beat an opponent 1v1 before passing or scoring.

4. Fun Soccer Game: "End Zone" (10 minutes)

- **Setup:** Mark two end zones on either side of the field.
- **Activity**: All players have a ball and must dribble past a defender (or the coach) who is in the middle, into the end zone to score. If the defender wins a ball they swap roles.
- **Progression:** Add more defenders or shrink the end zones as skills improve.

5. Small-Sided Game (10 minutes)

Wrap up with a game, encouraging players to apply their 1v1 skills!

Training Session Plan 5: Passing

1. Small-Sided Game (10 minutes)

Play a 4v4 game, encouraging kids to complete at least three passes before shooting.

2. Fun Soccer Game: "Pass and Follow" (10 minutes)

EIGHT TRAINING SESSION PLANS

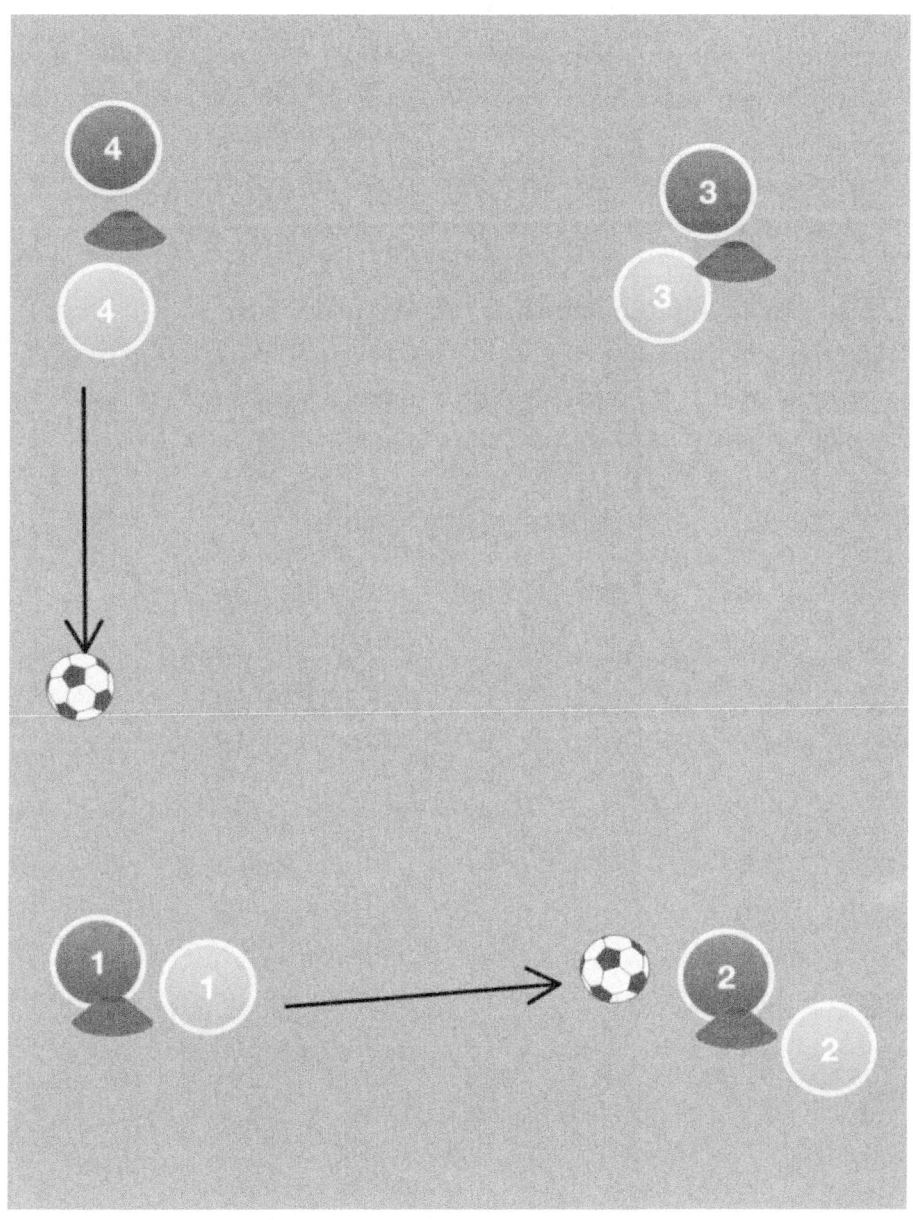

- **Setup:** Set up a square grid with cones at each corner.

- **Activity:** Players pass the ball to a teammate on the cone to their right and then run to that cone (following the ball). Continue until all players have rotated through a couple of times and then reverse the direction. Have two balls going at once for more advanced players.
- **Progression 1:** Use alternate feet when passing.
- **Progression 2:** Play a one two with the player you pass to.

3. Small-Sided Game Emphasising Passing (10 minutes)

Set up a 5v5 game and mark zones on the field (divide it into thirds or quarters or sixths). Players must pass to teammates in different zones 3 times before shooting **to encourage spreading out** and communication.

4. Fun Soccer Game: "Keep the Chain" (10 minutes)

EIGHT TRAINING SESSION PLANS

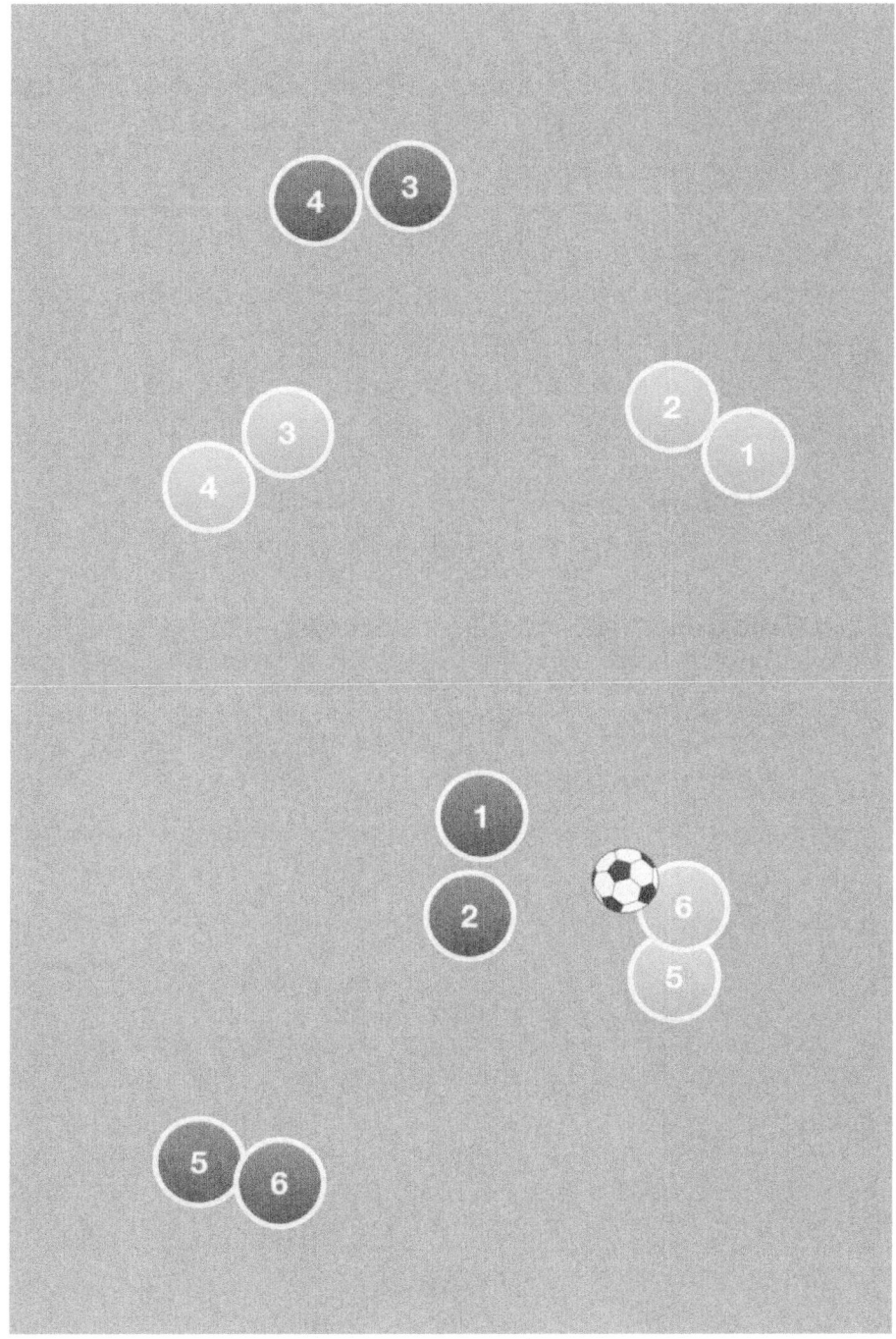

- **Setup:** In an area, have two teams with players forming chains by holding hands or linking arms.
- **Activity:** Chains of two or three players work together to pass the ball to teammates without breaking their chain. This is great for communication and team work as players must move together.

5. Small-Sided Game (10 minutes)

Finish with a free-play 4v4 game where players apply their passing skills. Offer encouragement for good teamwork and passing.

Training Session Plan 6: Dribbling

1. Small-Sided Game (10 minutes)

Begin with a 4v4 game and encourage players to dribble.

2. Fun Soccer Game: "Treasure Hunt" (10 minutes)

EIGHT TRAINING SESSION PLANS

- **Setup:** Scatter cones or small objects (treasures) around the field.
- **Activity:** Players dribble to collect as many treasures as they can within a time limit, carrying one treasure at a time back to their starting point. For example, spread 20 cones out in an area with yellow ones being worth 3 pieces of gold, red worth 2 pieces of gold and blue worth 1 piece of gold. Who can get the most points? Note: Hide a yellow cone or two under a blue one!

3. Small-Sided Game Emphasising Dribbling (10 minutes)

Play a 5v5 game with a rule: players must take at least three touches before passing or shooting. This encourages control and creativity.

4. Fun Soccer Game: "Sharks and Minnows" (10 minutes)

EIGHT TRAINING SESSION PLANS

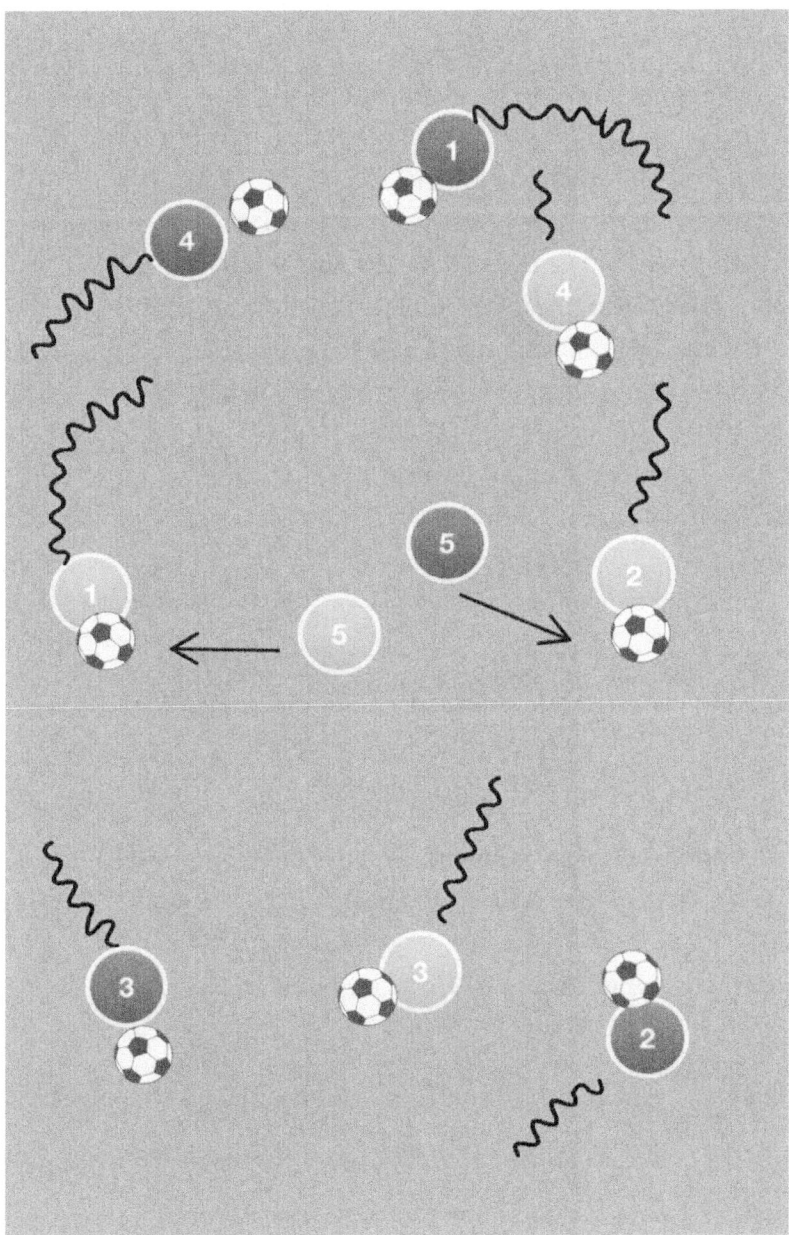

The two number 5's are the Sharks and must try to steal or kick the ball out from the Minnows. If a minnow loses their ball they become a Shark – play until there is one minnow left. Alternatively if a Minnow loses their ball to a Shark the players swap roles.

- **Setup:** One or two players (the sharks) try to steal the ball from others (the minnows) in a marked area.
- **Activity:** Minnows dribble to avoid losing their ball. If a shark steals their ball, the minnow become a shark too. Last minnow with a ball wins.
- **Alternative rules:** Have a couple of marked out 3x3 yard squares which are safe areas. The kids can dribble to these and stay on them for 5 seconds.
- Have it so that if a shark steals a minnows ball they swap roles (instead of all the minnows becoming sharks).

5. Small-Sided Game (10 minutes)

End with a small-sided game, praising players for using their dribbling skills and taking on opponents. High fives should be given out left, right and centre!

Training Session Plan 7: Shooting

1. Small-Sided Game (10 minutes)

Play a 4v4 game where players are encouraged to take quick shots on goal.

2. Fun Soccer Game: "Rapid Fire" (10 minutes)

EIGHT TRAINING SESSION PLANS

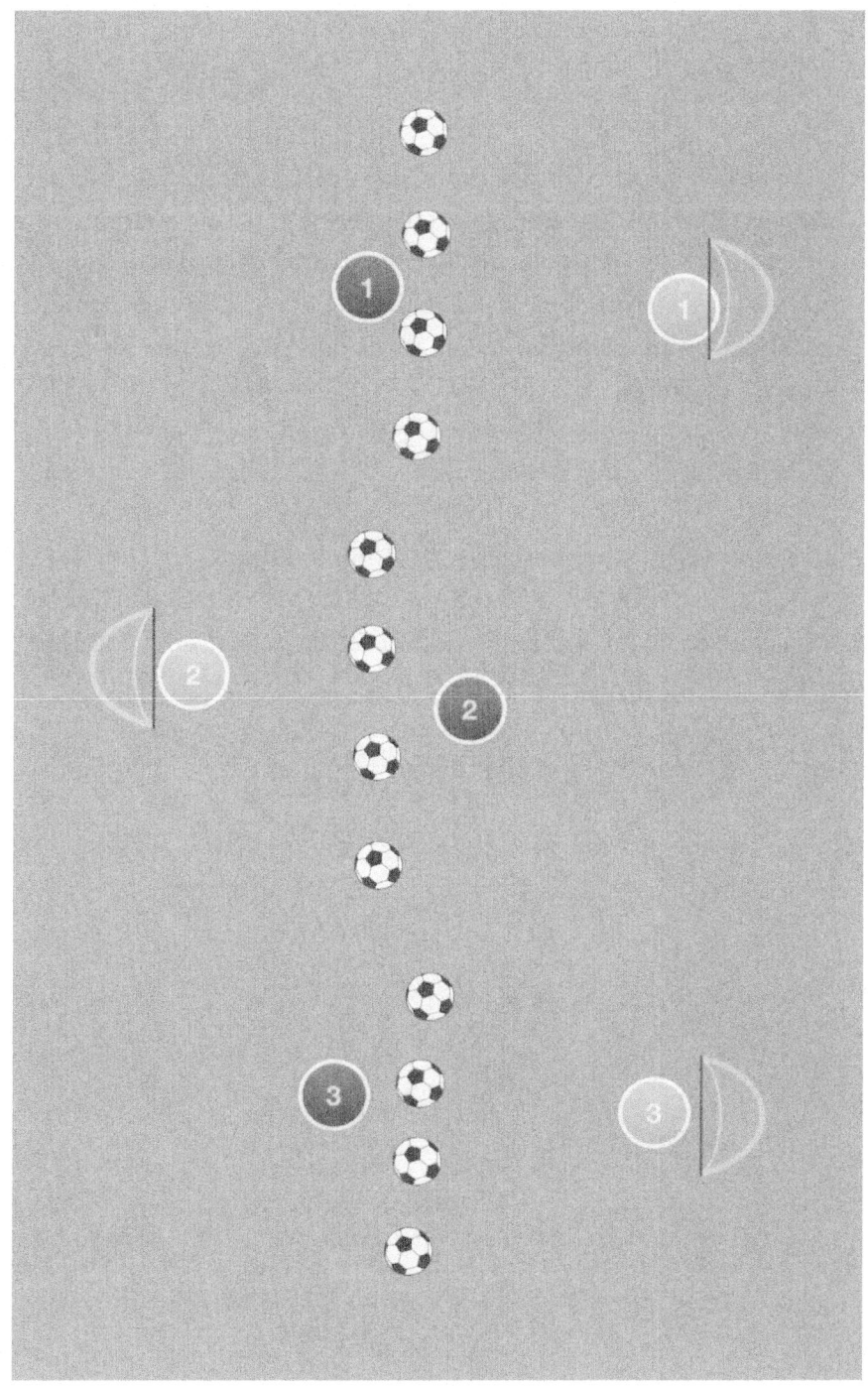

107

- **Setup:** Set up a line of four or five balls outside the penalty area. One goalkeeper stands in goal while one shooter stands at the edge of the area.
- **Activity:** The shooter must take quick shots, one after another, as fast as possible. This helps players learn as they can adjust after each shot and get muscle memory. After all balls are shot, switch the shooter and goalkeeper. Add a time limit (e.g., 10 seconds) to complete all shots for an extra challenge.
- Note: Try and have 2 or 3 mini goals set up and 2 or 3 players going at once so players aren't stood around.

3. Small-Sided Game Emphasising Shooting (10 minutes)

Play a 5v5 game with a rule: players must take a shot within five seconds of receiving the ball. This encourages quick decision-making and confidence in shooting.

4. Fun Soccer Game: "Power Shot Relay" (10 minutes)

EIGHT TRAINING SESSION PLANS

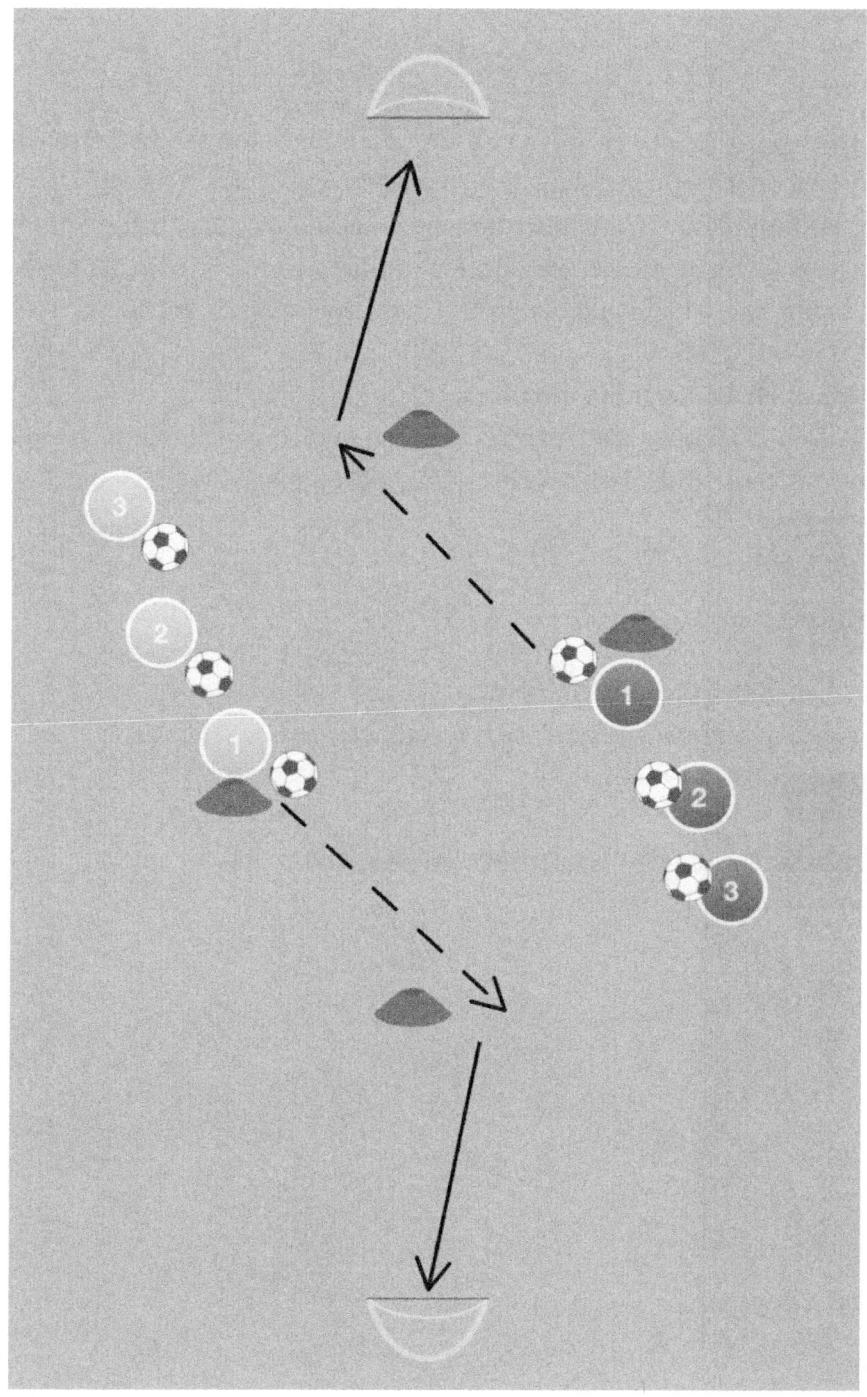

- **Setup:** Divide players into two teams. Set up a cone at a distance from the goal for each team (have a goal for each team).
- **Activity:** Players dribble to the cone, then shoot on goal before running back to tag the next teammate. First team to score a set number of goals wins. Play with or without goalkeepers depending on skill level.

5. Small-Sided Game (10 minutes)

End with a game where players focus on applying shooting techniques, cheering those who take creative or well-placed shots.

Training Session Plan 8: 1v1 Play

1. Small-Sided Game (10 minutes)

Play a 4v4 game with a rule: players must attempt at least one 1v1 move before passing or shooting.

2. Fun Soccer Game: "1v1 Battles" (10 minutes)

EIGHT TRAINING SESSION PLANS

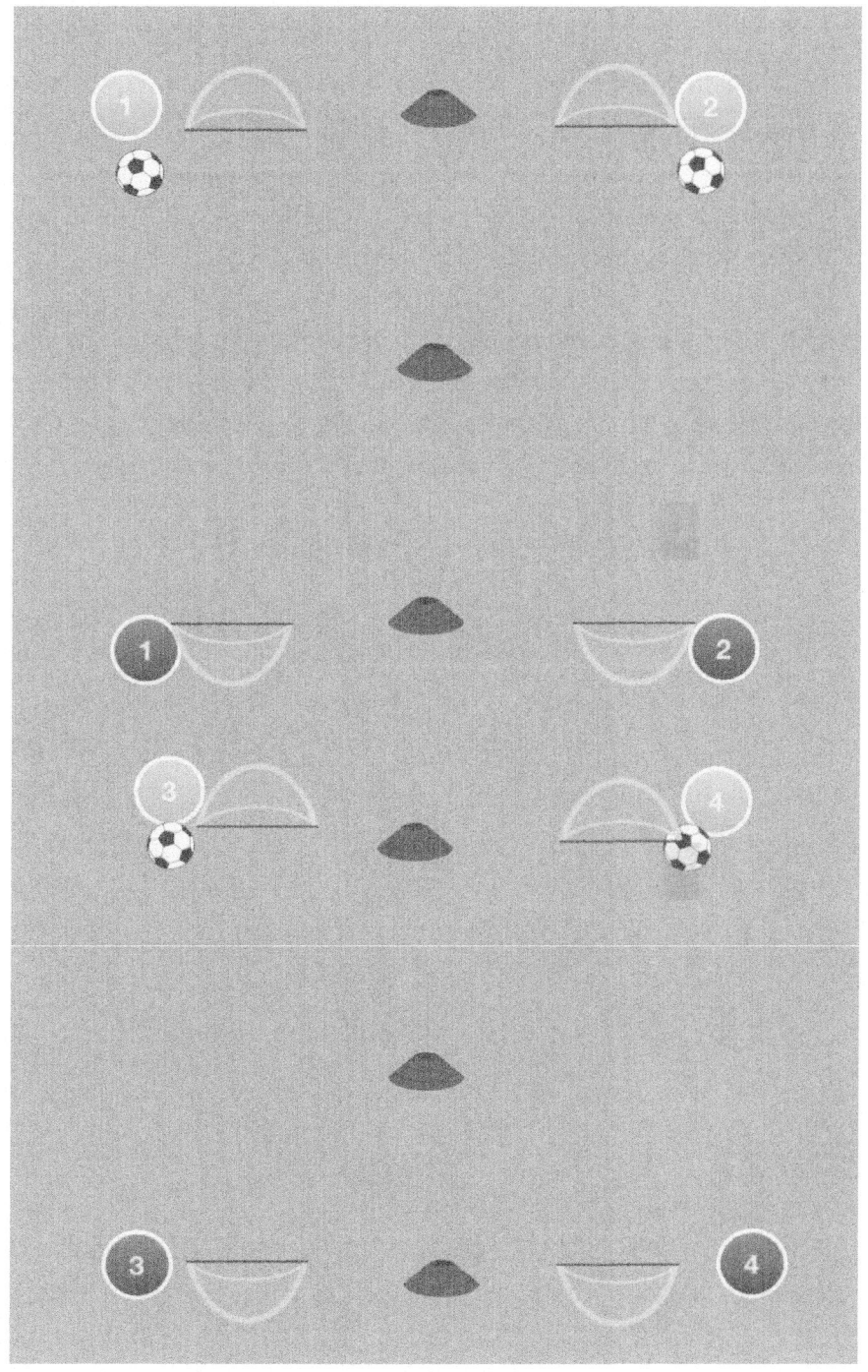

- **Setup:** Set up small grids with mini-goals on each end.
- **Activity:** Players compete 1v1 to dribble past their opponent and score in the mini-goal. Alternate the attacker and the defender. Because it is 1v1, players have no choice but to take on the defender.

3. Small-Sided Game Emphasising 1v1s (10 minutes)

Play a 5v5 game, encouraging players to use 1v1 moves to beat their opponents (shoulder drops, fakes, step overs, turns, change of pace or direction). Award extra points for successful take-ons leading to goals.

4. Fun Soccer Game: "1v1 Breakthrough" (10 minutes)

EIGHT TRAINING SESSION PLANS

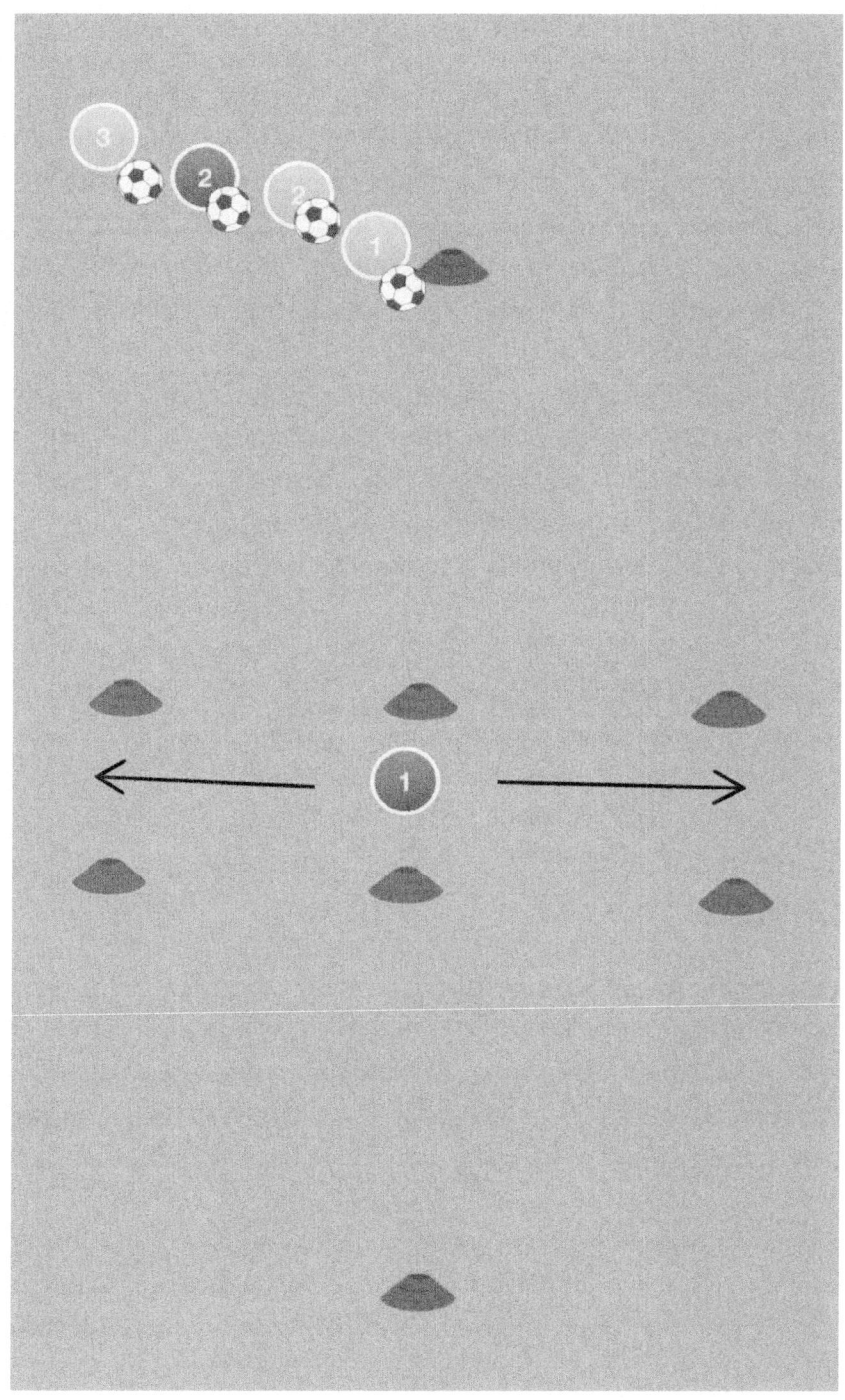

- **Setup:** Mark a small rectangular field (about 15x10 yards) with a "defender zone" in the middle. One attacker starts at one end with a ball, and one defender starts in the middle zone (they cannot leave this zone). The aim is for the attacker to dribble past the defender and reach the other end of the field. If successful they stay as an attacker and dribble back and rejoin the line.
- **Activity:** The attacker must use dribbling moves to beat the defender and cross the far line to score a point. If the defender wins the ball, they become an attacker, and a new defender rotates in.
- **Progression:** Shrink the playing area to force quicker decisions.
- Give attackers a time limit (e.g. 5 seconds) to beat their defender.

5. Small-Sided Game (10 minutes)

Finish with a game where players are rewarded for trying 1v1 skills, focusing on creativity and confidence in taking on opponents.

CONCLUSION

In this chapter, we've taken the guesswork out of planning training sessions by providing eight ready-to-use, fun, and effective practice plans. Covering key soccer fundamentals—**passing, dribbling, shooting, and 1v1 play**—these sessions are designed to help young players build their skills in an engaging and structured way.

Whether you're coaching once a week or mixing and matching drills, these sessions give you a solid foundation to run effective practices without the stress of planning from scratch. Just grab a session, set up the drills, and enjoy watching your players develop their confidence, teamwork, and love for the game. Coaching kids' soccer has never been easier!

9

TIPS FOR COACHING A BEGINNER GOALKEEPER IN SOCCER

Topics covered in "TIPS FOR COACHING A BEGINNER GOALKEEPER IN SOCCER"

1. **Start with the Basics of Positioning**
2. **Focus on Catching Technique**
3. **Teach Safe Diving and Ball Recovery**
4. **Work on Footwork and Reaction Time**
5. **Build Confidence with Encouragement**

This chapter is all about turning a beginners goalkeeper into a confident keeper by focusing on the essentials.

We'll begin by teaching them the basics of positioning, ensuring they know how to stand in the right place and "cut the angle" to reduce the shooter's chances. Next, we'll dive into proper catching techniques, showing them how to form the right hand shape for high balls and position their body perfectly for low ones.

From there, we'll introduce safe diving and ball recovery methods that help keep them protected while making effective saves. Quick and agile footwork is crucial too, so we'll work on drills to sharpen their reaction time and movement around the goal.

Finally, because confidence is key, we'll offer plenty of encouragement and practical tips to help them build self-belief in their abilities.

1. Start with the Basics of Positioning

- Teach the goalkeeper to stand in the middle of the goal and stay on their toes, ready to move in any direction.
- Explain the concept of "cutting the angle" by stepping forward to make the goal appear smaller to the shooter.
- *Tip:* Use cones to create a visual guide, showing where the keeper should stand depending on the ball's position. For example, put an arc of cones in front of the goalkeeper and then if the ball is coming from a certain position they move out to that cone.

2. Focus on Catching Technique

- Show them how to create a "W" shape with their hands (thumbs and index fingers touching) to catch high balls. Always bring the ball to the chest once they have control of it.
- For low balls, encourage them to get their body behind the ball to prevent it from slipping past. Don't just bend over from the hips with their legs apart. This may allow the ball to slip through the hands and then through the legs.
- *Drill:* Toss soft, easy balls to their hands and ground to build confidence and muscle memory.

3. Teach Safe Diving and Ball Recovery

- Encourage beginners to dive safely by practising on soft surfaces, focusing on landing on their side rather than their stomach or back.
- Demonstrate how to scoop the ball up with their hands when recovering low shots. Bringing the ball to their chest and holding it there, covering it with their arms and hands so it cannot be knocked out.
- *Drill:* Roll balls slowly to their left and right for them to dive and stop, gradually increasing the difficulty.

4. Work on Footwork and Reaction Time

- Quick feet are crucial for goalkeepers to get into position. Introduce ladder drills or side-to-side cone shuffles to build agility. You can set up a line of different coloured cones with the goalkeeper starting in the middle. Then call out a colour and they must quickly shuffle sideways to that colour.
- Reaction games, like calling out a number or colour of a cone for them to move toward and touch, can help improve their reflexes. Also starting on the ground and getting up as quickly as they can will help improve their goalkeeping.

5. Goal Kicks and Throwing

- Young children may not know that the goalkeeper usually takes the goal kicks, so run through practising some goal kicks at training. If the are a good kicker of the ball, get them to aim for a teammate. Or if they aren't so good, get them to aim towards the sides (away from the middle) so the ball doesn't get intercepted straight in front of goal.
- When they have the ball in the hands, they have the option to either kick it out from their hands or to throw it. So make sure to practice both options. Kicking out from their hands will come naturally to some and not to others, be patient and show them how to do it (drop the ball onto their foot, don't toss the ball up high). With throwing, they can either underarm it or overarm it so practice both techniques.

- Tip: You can set up cones at varying distances and angles for the goalkeeper to practise kicking or throwing to. Or set up a mini goal for them to aim at.

6. Build Confidence with Encouragement

- Goalkeeping can be intimidating, so focus on positive reinforcement. Praise their effort and improvement, not just saves.
- Let them participate in small-sided games as the goalkeeper to gain real-game experience in a low-pressure setting.
- *Tip:* Remind them it's okay to make mistakes—every save or miss is a chance to learn.

CONCLUSION

By focusing on these fundamentals and creating a supportive environment, beginner goalkeepers can develop confidence and enjoy learning this vital role!

If you'd like a free book, 50 TIPS ON HOW TO COACH A CHILDREN'S SOCCER TEAM - Ages 3 to 6 is available on Amazon permanently free.

Special Offer – Online Kids Coaching Course

As a reader of this book, you can get my *Coaching Kids Soccer* course on Udemy at a discounted price.

☞ Use this link to access the discount: https://rebrand.ly/kidscourse

10

BASIC UNDERSTANDING OF KIDS SOCCER RULES AND GUIDELINES

Topics covered in "BASIC UNDERSTANDING OF KIDS SOCCER RULES AND GUIDELINES"

1. **Basic Understanding of Kids Soccer Rules and Guidelines**

Children's soccer is designed to be simple and fun, with rules adapted to suit young players' needs. I listed some guidelines in an earlier chapter (see below) which I expand on here.

Some main rules/regulations for an Under 7/8's Football league:

- **Format** 5v5
- **Match Length** 20 mins each way.
- **Pitch Size** 40 yd x 30 yd
- **Ball Size** 3
- **Substitutions** Roll-off roll-on substitutions (also called interchange) can be made at any time during the game with permission from the referee, including players who have already been substituted.

- **Throw-ins** Traditional throw-ins are part of the rules, but referees may allow players to try again if they use incorrect technique.
- **Offside** There is no offside.
- **Playing Equipment** Shin pads are mandatory. These should be covered entirely by knee-length socks.

1. Simplified Rules:

Smaller team sizes: Games are usually 3v3, 4v4, 5v5, 6v6, 7v7 for younger kids to ensure everyone gets plenty of touches on the ball. This helps speed up skill development.

At training, use mini-tournaments with multiple small-sided games to keep everyone involved (as opposed to one big game of 8v8 where players don't get many touches).

Shorter game durations: For kids aged 5-10, halves/quarters might last 10-15 minutes, with a break in between to keep energy levels up.

Have a snack and drink during the break to keep young bodies and spirits high.

Rule modifications: Avoid strict enforcement of rules, like throw-in techniques, at younger levels. Let kids learn through play and demonstrating rules visually—like stepping over a line for a throw-in—to make them easier for the children to grasp.

2. Focus on Safety:

Proper equipment: Make sure kids wear shin pads under their socks and well-fitted boots. Keep spare shin pads in your bag for kids who might forget theirs (I coach adults as well and always make sure to have a spare pair for those forgetful players - Henry Cook I'm talking to you!)

Enforce safe play: Teach kids to avoid dangerous behaviours like slide tackles. *Prioritise safety over competition.* Yes, we want players to be brave, compete for the ball and to get "stuck in", but make sure to keep it under control.

Field inspection: Before every session, check the field for hazards like rocks, pot holes, or broken glass. Also, make sure the training area isn't too close to a car park or road - we obviously don't want kiddies chasing a ball onto a road.

Conclusion

No one expects you to know all the rules and guidelines when it comes to kids soccer. But just polish up on the main rules and you will learn the rest as you go!

11

GAME DAY ESSENTIALS

Topics covered in "GAME DAY ESSENTIALS"

1. **Preparing for Match Day**
2. **Managing the Game: Organising Line-Ups and Substitutions**
3. **Post-Game Wrap-Up**
4. **Bonus Tips for Game Day Success**

Game day is one of the most exciting parts of children's soccer. You need to be prepared, organised and remember to make it a positive experience for your players. With the right approach (using my advice below!), you can make it a fun and rewarding time for players, parents, and yourself.

1. Preparing for Match Day

1. Organise Equipment:

Always ensure you have the essentials: soccer balls to warm up with, cones, bibs/pinnies, a whistle, water bottles, spare shin pads, and a first-aid kit.

Tip 1: Label all soccer balls with your name or the team name to prevent mix-ups with other teams.

Tip 2: Invest in a portable wagon or large bag to carry your gear easily.

Tip 3: **Create a "game day checklist"** on your phone or match day notepad so you can pack everything the night before.

2. Communicate with Parents:

Provide all the match details at least a few days in advance: time, location, and any additional instructions (Is it hard to find the ground? Are you car pooling? Is it astro turf so bring different boots?).

Example: "Please arrive by 9:30 AM for our 10:00 AM match. Bring a water bottle, shin guards, and wear your red kit."

Use group messaging apps like TeamSnap or WhatsApp for quick updates.

Tip: Send a reminder the night before and also a few hours before the match to ensure everyone is on the same page. It's better to be safe than to be short on players due to parents reading the kick off time or location incorrectly.

3. Pre-Game Warm-Up:

Begin with light jogging and dynamic stretches to get players physically and mentally ready.

> *Note: If you have slightly older players (8,9,10 year olds) you could introduce them to the FIFA 11. This is an approved warm-up that is shown to reduce injuries and get players football muscles activated. I won't go into detail here but if you search "FIFA 11 football warm-up" you will be able to find some videos that show you what it involves. I use it with all my adult teams.*

Example: Use fun stretches like "soccer lunges" where kids hold a ball while doing lunges.

Incorporate short, engaging drills to build focus. Drills like "passing triangles" (three players passing and moving) or "dribble and shoot" (set up 3 or 4 cones that players dribble through before shooting on goal) are effective for warming up key skills. At young ages, kids won't focus for a long warm up, so it's best to keep it to 15-20 minutes.

Game Idea: Play "Traffic Jam" where players dribble around cones spread out randomly in a large circle while avoiding each other.

Tip: Keep warm-ups short (15-20 minutes) but structured, and include a team huddle before kick off to reinforce positivity and teamwork.

Tip: Rondos (similar to piggy in the middle) are a great pre-game drill. You can do it in a small area. Everyone can have a minute in the middle trying to win the ball and all the other players get plenty of touches on the ball. Plus there should be lots of talking and calling out for the ball during a rondo.

> Note: I have two books on rondos available on Amazon "Soccer Rondos Volume 1 and 2".

2. Managing the Game: Organising line-ups and substitutions

1. Plan Ahead:

Create a line-up on your notepad before match day that outlines starting positions and player rotations for each half or quarter. Make it clear who you intend to come off and be replaced with, so then you can leave a parent or assistant in charge of the rotations if you want to.

For example: *End of first quarter - Smithy off - Jason on (Jason goes to right back).*

Note: You will find a match day template at the end of this chapter. There is a template with four soccer pitches on it, so if you play four quarters you can put your intended starting line-up for that quarter on each one.

Tip: Prepare alternative starting line-ups in case players arrive late.

2. Rotate Positions:

Allow players to experience different roles on the field to broaden their understanding of the game and develop diverse skills.

Example: Rotate defenders into midfield roles during the second half to challenge their decision-making and ball control. Defenders have most of the play in front of them, but midfielders must be more aware of who is behind and beside them. Plus they have less time to make decisions in midfield.

Example: "Andrew, you'll start as goalie today, and then we'll move you to forward in the second half."

Tip: Take mental notes during the game to identify players' strengths in various roles and provide feedback after.

Ensure fair playing time by rotating players regularly. Kids value their time on the field.

Tip: Use a whiteboard, app or pen and paper to mark down who's playing and for how long. Assign a parent to help manage substitutions and game time if possible.

Note: Sometime a coach can take on too much responsibility and think they have to do everything themselves. This isn't true and can be detrimental and reduce your enjoyment of your role. If parents or older siblings are willing to help, take them up on it! Many hands make light work.

3. Consider Player Strengths:

Put players in positions that suit their current skill level. You can mix it up when they've gained confidence in their current position.

Example: Place a confident and vocal player as a central defender to organise the back line, while a speedy player might do best as a winger.

Tip: Use practices to identify each player's strengths and preferences.

4. Communicate the Plan:

Share the line-up with players before the game starts to avoid confusion.

Example: Gather the team for a quick briefing, using a whiteboard or drawing in the dirt to show positions.

Note: I sometimes place cones representing the line-up before the game in a small area of the pitch or on the change room floor. Green as the defenders, yellow as the midfield and red as the attackers. Then the players can clearly see where they are on the pitch and it becomes clearer in their mind.

Another way is if players bring their own drink bottles, in a small area place their drink bottles in the positions they are starting. This way they see their drink bottle and know this is where they should be on the field.

Tip: Remind players they may switch positions if needed to help the team.

5. Adjust as Needed:

Be ready to change the line-up during the game based on fatigue, performance, or how the opposition play.

Example: If the opposing team has a strong striker, move an experienced defender to mark them more closely. Or if a player has run out of gas and you don't have any extra players, rest them up front or in defence and tell them not to make any big runs if they can help it.

6. Celebrate Effort in All Positions:

Praise players for their contributions regardless of position. Highlight how every role is crucial to the team's success.

Example: "Great job holding the midfield, Sam! You really stopped a lot of attacks getting through to the defenders."

Another pet peeve of mine is the goal scorers getting all the credit. The opportunity for the striker to score may have come about because a defender made a great tackle or interception. Then they made a great pass to the striker. So make sure to celebrate what happened earlier in the play.

Tip: Rotate feedback to ensure players in less glamorous roles, like defenders or goalkeepers, feel equally valued.

7. Encouraging Teamwork:

Cheer on players for their effort, teamwork, and smart decisions, not just for scoring goals.

Example: "Great job, Karen, for passing to an open teammate instead of trying to dribble through the defenders!"

Teach players to communicate on the field with simple phrases like "Here!", "Turn!" or "Man on!" during play.

Tip: Practice these phrases during training so they become second nature on game day.

8. Handling Challenges:

Mistakes while playing soccer are inevitable, but they're also learning opportunities. Stay calm and guide players constructively.

Example: "It's okay that we missed that pass—next time, let's try keeping our heads up to spot open teammates."

Manage emotional parents by modelling calm behaviour. If a parent becomes overly vocal, address them respectfully after the game.

If bad parent behaviour continues on more than one occasion, knock it on the head the second time. Simply tell the parent they are no longer welcome at the game until they change their behaviour and the game will not go ahead if they are there. You (the coach) are just like a referee - you are doing your best and deserve respect.

Tip: Set clear guidelines for parent behaviour at the start of the season to prevent conflicts. Some parents haven't been involved with sport before - or team sports - so they may not know how best to act around childrens sport.

3. Post-Game Wrap-Up

1. Team Talk:

Gather the team immediately after the game for a quick talk. Highlight their hard work and specific moments of success.

Example: "I loved how everyone worked hard on defence today, especially during that tricky second half."

Tip: Avoid dwelling on mistakes; instead, frame feedback around improvement opportunities.

2. Thank Opponents and Referees:

Sportsmanship is non-negotiable. Teach players to shake hands with opponents and thank referees with sincerity.

Example: Lead by example, saying, "Thanks for officiating today ref!" and encourage players to do the same.

3. Celebrate Progress:

Recognize individual and team achievements with small awards or shout outs.

Example: Hand out certificates for "Player of the Match" with categories like "Best Defender" or "Most Encouraging Teammate." I have a set of certificates available for free on my website that you can print out -www.chriskingsoccercoach.com or email me at chriskingsoccercoach@gmail.com and I'll send them through to you. I always like to hear from coaches!

Tip: Rotate awards to ensure every player feels celebrated over the course of the season.

Bonus: Share positive observations with parents to keep them engaged and supportive. For instance, "Shaun showed great focus on defence today—he's really improving!"

4. Bonus Tips for Game Day Success

Bring Snacks: Kids often need a quick energy boost after the game. Coordinate with parents to provide fruit slices or muesli bars.

Stay Positive, Win, Lose or Draw: Remember, the goal is development and enjoyment. Show resilience and positivity, especially after a tough game.

Example: "The score doesn't matter—what matters is how we supported each other out there."

Capture the Moments: Assign a parent to take photos or videos during the game to share with the team later. These memories help build camaraderie and excitement for future matches.

CONCLUSION

With preparation and a focus on fun and improvement, game days can become a fantastic experiences for players, parents, and coaches alike. As a coach, you have the opportunity to give the children positive experiences and lessons that they can take with them through out their lives. I still remember games from my youth and are good friends with who I played soccer with at an early age.

_____ v _____   **DATE** _____

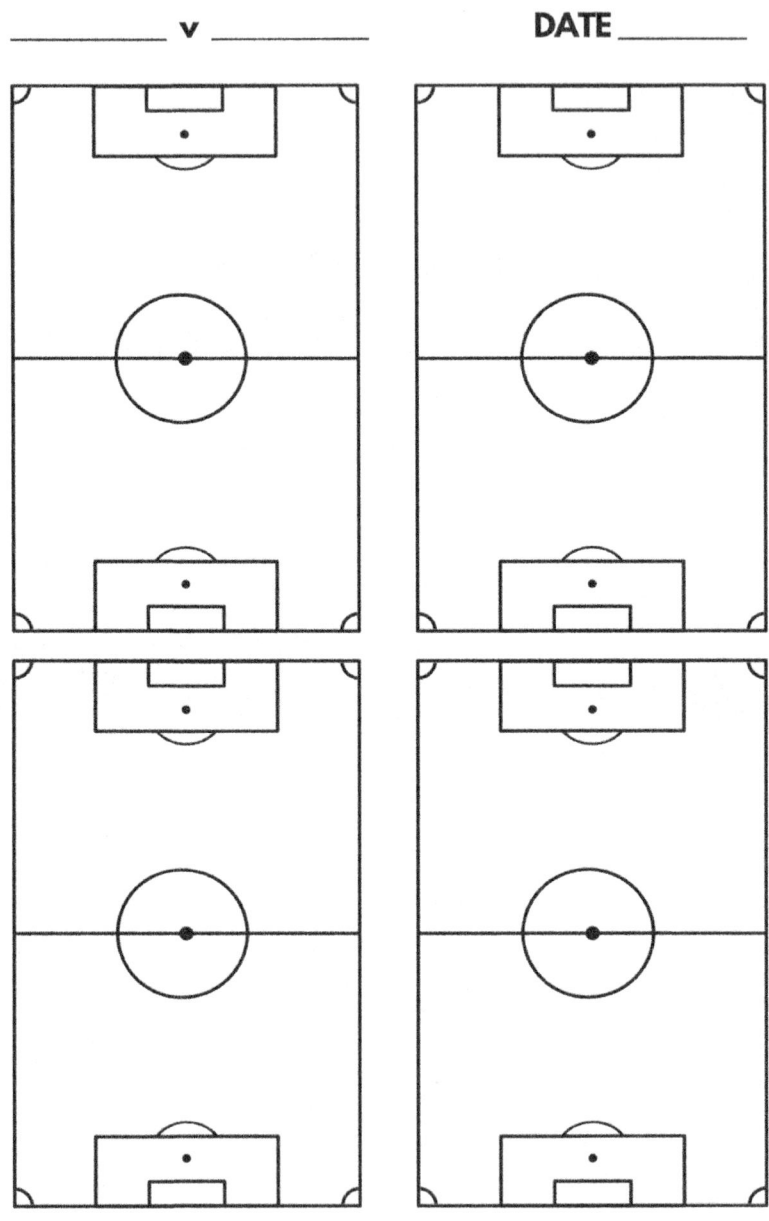

GAME DAY ESSENTIALS

_____ v _____   **DATE** _____

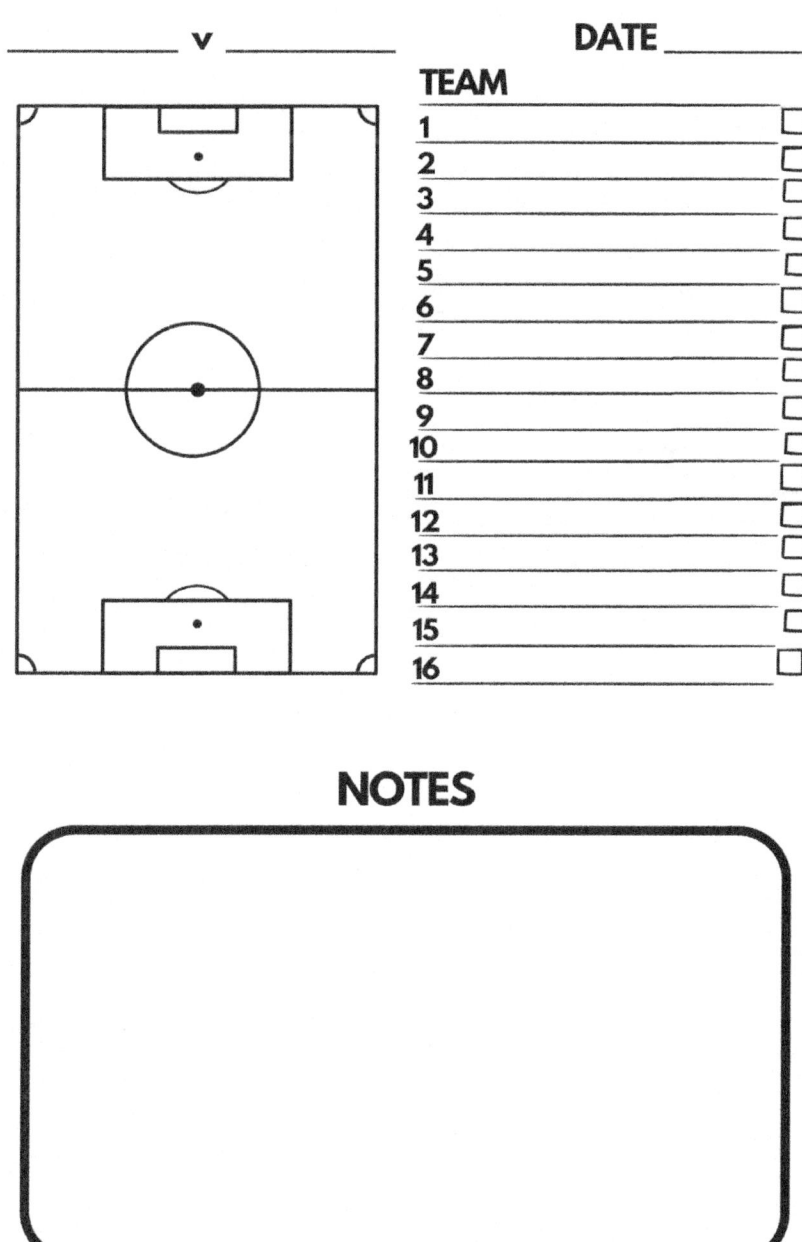

TEAM
1 _____ ☐
2 _____ ☐
3 _____ ☐
4 _____ ☐
5 _____ ☐
6 _____ ☐
7 _____ ☐
8 _____ ☐
9 _____ ☐
10 _____ ☐
11 _____ ☐
12 _____ ☐
13 _____ ☐
14 _____ ☐
15 _____ ☐
16 _____ ☐

NOTES

CONGRATULATIONS ON YOUR DEDICATION IN SOCCER!

SOCCER CERTIFICATE
PLAYER OF THE GAME

This certificate recognizes your exceptional skills and commitment to the sport. Keep chasing your soccer dreams. Congratulations!

COACH/TEACHER

12

FORMATIONS FOR KIDS SOCCER TEAMS (BY AGE GROUP)

Topics covered in "FORMATIONS FOR KIDS SOCCER TEAMS (BY AGE GROUP)"

1. **5–6 Year Olds: Keep it simple (3v3 or 4v4)**
2. **7–8 Year Olds: Introduce basic positions (5v5 or 6v6)**
3. **9–10 Year Olds: Structured play (7v7)**
4. **General tips for all age groups**

When coaching young players, formations should focus on simplicity, and maximizing involvement. The goal is to ensure every child gets plenty of touches on the ball while learning basic positional play. Here are some practical formation tips for different age groups:

1. 5–6 Year Olds: Keep It Simple (3v3 or 4v4)

At this age, kids are just beginning to understand the concept of positions, and the focus should be on letting them explore the game and have fun.

- **Recommended Formation:**

- *No specific positions. Just let them play.*
- **Key Tips:**
- Avoid rigid positioning since very young kids will naturally chase the ball.
- Focus on spacing by encouraging them not to "crowd the ball." Use cones in practice to show the areas they should stay in.
- Rotate roles often to let every child experience different parts of the game.
- **Why This Works:** Smaller teams keep everyone involved and help kids develop fundamental dribbling and passing skills without worrying about complex tactics.

2. 7–8 Year Olds: Introduce Basic Positions (5v5 or 6v6)

Kids in this age group are ready to understand basic roles like defender, midfielder, and attacker. Formations should encourage teamwork and passing.

- **Recommended Formation:**
- *For 5v5:* 2-2 (2 defenders, 2 attacker).
- *For 6v6:* 2-2-1 (2 defenders, 2 midfielders, 1 attacker).
- **Key Tips:**
- Use clear instructions for roles: Defenders stay back to protect the goal, midfielders help in both attack and defence, and attackers focus on scoring.
- Teach the idea of spacing, using the phrase "spread out and look for teammates to receive the ball from or pass to."
- Introduce basic shape concepts, like a triangle or diamond, to help players understand passing lanes and movement.
- **Why This Works:** These formations are balanced, simple, and teach kids the importance of both offence and defence.

3. 9–10 Year Olds: Structured Play (7v7)

At this age, kids can handle more structure, including roles and formations, while still keeping the game fun and accessible.

- **Recommended Formation:**
- *For 7v7: 2-3-1 (2 defenders, 3 midfielders, 1 attacker)*
- *Alternative: 3-2-1 (3 defenders, 2 midfielders, 1 attacker)*
- **Key Tips:**
- Explain how defenders, midfielders, and attackers work together as a team. Use simple terms like "defenders stay back," "midfielders move up and down," and "attackers press forward."
- Encourage midfielders to support both the attack and defence, helping them learn to transition.
- Introduce the concept of staying in their "zone" to maintain team shape without overwhelming them with strict tactics.
- Rotate positions during practices and games so all players learn different roles.
- **Why This Works:** This formation gives structure while allowing players to work on teamwork, spacing, and understanding their responsibilities.

General Tips for All Age Groups

1. **Emphasise Fun Over Structure:** Especially for younger age groups, avoid rigid formations and focus on giving kids the freedom to enjoy the game.
2. **Use Visual Aids:** Mark out zones or use cones during practice to help players understand positioning.
3. **Keep Everyone Involved:** Avoid assigning one player as a permanent goalkeeper or limiting kids to one role for too long.

CONCLUSION

By using age-appropriate formations and keeping things simple, you'll help kids build their skills and confidence while learning the importance of playing their role inside a team.

13

BUILDING TEAM SPIRIT AND CONFIDENCE

Topics covered in "BUILDING TEAM SPIRIT and CONFIDENCE"

1. **Motivating Young Players**
2. **Dealing with Setbacks and Mistakes**
3. **Positive Communication Strategies**

Players that enjoy playing together help create an enjoyable soccer season. Here's how to create a positive environment that brings out the best in your players!

1. Motivating Young Players

1. Set Team Goals:
Encourage players to work toward shared objectives, like improving passing accuracy, defending as a group, or maintaining a positive attitude throughout games.
   Example 1: "Let's aim to complete five passes in a row during today's

match!"

Example 2: If your team let's a goal in, make sure they go and give their keeper a pat on the back and say it's ok.

Break larger goals into achievable milestones to keep players motivated and focused.

Example: Celebrate when the team improves their communication on the field. Say "Well done!" when they do such things as calling for the ball or warning teammates about opponents.

Bonus: Create themed goals, like "Defence Week," where the team focuses specifically on defensive organisation.

2. Celebrate Effort:

Reward players for giving their best, ***regardless of the outcome***. Focus on hard work and improvement.

Example: "I loved how you kept trying to win the ball back after losing it—great effort Tommy!"

Tip: Create a "player effort jar" where tokens (bottle tops, pennies, buttons) are added for each act of hustle or determination during a game or practice. Review the jar's progress weekly and celebrate reaching a full jar with a team activity. You would be surprised how something like this works. Rather than just words, the children can see something physical (the player effort jar) and it filling up as they do what you encourage them to do.

Use stickers as tangible reminders of their effort.

Example: Award stickers after practice or a game with phrases like "Great Effort!" or "Team Player" to reinforce positive behaviours. It's a small thing but it can really stay in a young players mind and encourages them to keep improving.

3. Make It Fun:

I know I sound like a Beach Boys song here, but soccer at a young age is all about fun fun fun. So incorporate fun games and challenges into practice to keep players engaged, excited and build team spirit.

Game Idea: Create a "goal-scoring contest" where players earn points for creative finishes or creative teamwork leading to a goal. At this young age, player creativity should be encouraged! Let them try a back heel, a scissor kick, a step over or something they invented.

Tip: Add variety by including small-sided games, obstacle courses, or relay races that incorporate soccer skills.

Surprise players occasionally with themed practices, like "World Cup Day," where each small team represents a different country.

A fun game is "Pirate Soccer," where players dribble to find hidden "treasure" (cones or objects) scattered around the field. You can place hidden "gold" under cones by putting some yellow cones underneath other coloured ones and see who can find the gold first or who can collect the most cones. The player that finds the most gold cones can choose the next game or can be called "King" "Queen" or "Pirate" for the rest of training.

Additional Example: Incorporate themed practices, like "Superhero Day," where players pretend to have superpowers while playing.

Additional Tip: Encourage creativity by allowing kids to invent their own games during practice.

4. Provide Positive Reinforcement:

Use specific praise to highlight what players are doing well.

Example: "Your positioning today was fantastic—you really helped close down their attacks and not allow them to get into the box."

Tip: Focus on the effort, even if the execution wasn't perfect. For instance, "I loved how you tried to stay wide on the wing—that's exactly what we're looking for."

Celebrate small wins during games, like a player successfully making a challenging pass or tracking back to defend.

Bonus: Create "praise breaks" during practices, where the team pauses to acknowledge great plays or acts of teamwork.

2. Dealing with Setbacks and Mistakes

1. Normalise Mistakes:

Mention that mistakes are part of learning and even the best players make them.

Example: Share stories of famous players who overcame setbacks, like Lionel Messi being told he was too small or a top player missing a decisive penalty in a major tournament (Roberto Baggio).

Tip: Use your own experiences to relate. "When I played, I remember missing an open goal. But for the next 10 minutes I worked harder than I ever had, chasing down every one. I forced a mistake from a defender and I scored a goal only 10 minutes after I made a mistake."

Additional Example: Show a video on your phone of a professional player making a mistake but recovering brilliantly.

Additional Tip: Use phrases like, "Mistakes mean you're trying and learning."

2. Use mistakes as teaching moments to discuss what could be done differently next time.

Tip: Say, **"What did we learn from that?"** instead of "Why did you do that?"

Example: "That was a tough pass to make—next time, try looking for a closer teammate."

3. Encourage a Growth Mindset:

A growth mindset is **the belief that your talents and intelligence can be developed through effort, learning, and persistence**.

People with a growth mindset:

1. See challenges as opportunities to learn
2. Persist in the face of setbacks
3. Learn from criticism
4. Find inspiration in the success of others
5. Are always looking for ways to improve

Re-read the 5 points above because they are very important for young players to gain confidence and improve.

Focus on effort and improvement rather than the players natural talent.
   Example: "I can see you're getting better at controlling the ball—keep practising, and it'll feel natural soon!"
   Tip: Reinforce the concept that practice leads to progress by comparing their current skills to where they were at the start of the season.

Highlight improvement over time by reminding players of how far they've come.
   Example: "Remember when we struggled to make three passes in a row? Now we're completing five or six every game!"
   Bonus: Create "before and after" moments by recording short clips of players' skills at the start and midway through the season. Get a parent to film if you're busy coaching. These can have a big impact on motivating young players to get practising. They can see that they have improved so it motivates them even more.

4. Stay Positive After Losses:
   Highlight the team's effort and identify areas to build on in future games.
   Example: "We may not have won, but our teamwork improved so much—let's keep working on it!"

Focus on individual successes, such as a player's improved defensive positioning or creative dribbling.

Tip: Always end post-game talks with something positive to leave players feeling motivated for the next match.

Example: "Bainey's passing today really helped us create chances, and the defence worked so well together!"

3. Positive Communication Strategies

1. Be a Role Model:

Demonstrate respectful communication by speaking calmly and encouragingly, *even in high-pressure situations*.

Tip: Use phrases like "Let's work on this together" instead of pointing out flaws. For example, "Next time, let's try staying wider on the wing to stretch the defence."

Example: "I liked how you tried that tricky move! Keep practising it, and it'll work better next time."

2. Encourage Teammates To Support Each Other:

Teach players to lift each other up with positive comments.

Example: "Nice pass!" or "Great save!" during games and practices.

Tip: Create a team tradition where players share compliments during post-game talks.

Example: Have each player say one nice thing about a teammate after every game or practice.

Bonus: During drills, encourage players to clap or cheer when someone completes a tough challenge.

3. Use the Sandwich Method:

When giving constructive feedback, sandwich it between two positive comments.

Example: "Your hustle was great today! Next time, let's work on keeping the ball closer while dribbling. Keep up the great energy!"

Tip: End with an action plan, such as "We'll focus on this during our next practice."

4. Build Trust Through Open Communication:

Encourage players to share their thoughts and feelings about the game or practice. This can bring shy players out of their shell. Plus it helps create leaders and 'buy in' to what you are trying to achieve.

Example: "What was your favourite part of today's game?" or "What do you think we can improve on as a team?"

Tip: Make time for one-on-one chats with players to understand their individual needs and goals. This is very important. It's easy for the coach to get caught up in training, match days and communicating with parents etc. But at the end of the day your role as a coach is to encourage, improve and listen to your players.

So even if it's during training, make time. Sometimes I'll have a small sided game going at training and I'll pull one player out at a time and have a chat with them for a few minutes.

Bonus: Hold occasional "team circles," where players and coaches discuss the highs and lows of recent games openly.

CONCLUSION

Building team spirit and confidence takes time, but the results are worth it. By motivating your players, helping them learn from setbacks, and encouraging positive communication, you'll create an environment where everyone thrives and have smiles on their faces when they're at football! And that's exactly what we want - even if your players have had a rough day at school (or work or home), when they get to soccer you want them to have a smile on their face and enjoying themselves.

14

PARENT AND VOLUNTEER ENGAGEMENT

Topics covered in "PARENT and VOLUNTEER ENGAGEMENT"

1. **Collaborating with parents**
2. **Recruiting and training assistants**
3. **Managing parent expectations**
4. **Additional tips for parent and volunteer engagement**

Parents and volunteers play a vital role in the success of a kids soccer team. By collaborating effectively, recruiting and training helpers, and managing expectations, you can create an environment that helps young soccer players and makes your job as a coach easier and more enjoyable.

1. Collaborating with Parents

1. Set Clear Expectations

Most of the things mentioned below won't arise, but being being pro-active and bringing them up early in the season, you will reduce the chances of parent misbehaviour.

Host a parent meeting at the start of the season to outline your coaching philosophy, team rules, and expectations. This can just be a 15-30 minute meeting before or after training on one of the first nights. A good idea is to have a pizza night after training so the kids can enjoy a pizza and you can have a chat with the parents.

Example: "Our focus this season is on effort, learning, and teamwork—not just winning. Let's cheer for all the kids and keep the sidelines positive."

Provide an email summary that includes practice schedules, game times, and contact information.

Tip: Create a "Parent Code of Conduct" document that emphasises sportsmanship and support. Below is an example that you could use:

2. Parent Code of Conduct for Kids Soccer Teams

Here is an example of a code of conduct that you could email to parents or printout and hand out before the season starts:

> *"As a parent, your role is essential in encouraging a positive and supportive environment for all our young soccer players. We would love for you to show good sportsmanship, cheer positively for all players, and respect coaches, referees, and opponents. Refrain from coaching from the sidelines and allow the players to enjoy the game and learn at their own pace.*
>
> *Celebrate effort and improvement over winning, and always remember that this is about the kids' growth, fun, and love for the game. Together, we can create a supportive environment that inspires our young athletes to thrive both on and off the field".*

- **Additional Example:** Prepare a handout listing dos and don'ts for sideline behaviour, like "Cheer positively; don't coach from the sidelines."

- Additional Tip: Emphasise how positive parental involvement enhances their child's experience.

3. Encourage Positive Sideline behaviour:

Teach parents how to support players constructively during games.

Example: "Cheer for effort, not just goals." 'Great hustle!' or 'Nice teamwork!'"

Tip: Share examples of positive sideline cheers versus critical comments.

Additional Example: Create a "Parent Pledge" that includes commitments to respect referees and encourage all players. You could get the parents to acknowledge the "Parent Code Of Conduct" I provided above. Email it to them and ask for them to email it back agreeing to adhere to it. This way, if you have issues during the season with parents misbehaving you can remind them of the pledge they agreed to.

Additional Tip: Address concerns privately if negative behaviours arise, **focusing on solutions.** During a game is not the time to get in a discussion with an aggrieved parent.

4. Encourage Open Communication:

Encourage parents to ask questions and share concerns respectfully.

Example: "If you ever have questions about your child's development or playing time, feel free to chat with me after practice or send me an email."

Use a team messaging app like WhatsApp to provide quick updates and reminders, this way parents will be "in the loop" of what you are trying to achieve.

Tip: Send weekly messages highlighting the team's **goals, achievements, and areas of focus.** This shows that you have the children's best interest at heart and are looking to develop them.

5. Involve Parents in Team Activities:

Invite parents to help with tasks like organising snacks, arranging carpools, or taking photos/videos during games.

Example: "We need volunteers to set up chairs and bring half-time snacks for our game this Saturday. Let me know if you can help!"

Additional Example: Invite parents to assist with warm-ups or simple drills if they're comfortable doing this. It's a great way to get buy in from them and it shows them the amount of work and time that a coach puts into a team.

Additional Tip: Rotate responsibilities to ensure all parents have opportunities to participate.

Create opportunities for parents to bond with each other, like a casual "meet and greet" after practice. You could do this once a month. Have tea and coffee in the clubrooms or go to a local cafe or park.

Tip: Use these events to reinforce the team's values and goals in a relaxed setting.

6. Recognise Parental Contributions:

Show appreciation for parents' efforts throughout the season.

Example: Send thank-you emails or organise a "Parent Appreciation Day" where kids write thank-you notes to their parents.

Tip: Mention specific contributions, like "Thanks to Annie's dad for washing and bringing the kit last week!"

2. Recruiting and Training Assistants

1. Identify Helpers Early:

Ask parents during the preseason meeting if they'd like to assist with coaching or team management. Some will and some won't, but you won't know until you ask.

Example: "We're looking for a couple of assistant coaches to help set up drills and manage substitutions during games. Let me know if you're interested!"

Look for parents who have soccer experience or a willingness to learn.

Tip: **Emphasise that prior coaching experience isn't necessary**—enthusiasm and dependability are what matter most! A lot of people are worried that they need to be a soccer expert and watch five Premier League games each weekend - tell them this is not the case.

Tip: Be clear about the time commitment and responsibilities.

Additional Example: Approach parents directly at practices and games to see if they're interested.

Additional Tip: Highlight the benefits, like learning new skills, meeting other coaches at the club/school and contributing to the team's success.

> *A great starting point for them would be my online coaching course HOW TO COACH KIDS SOCCER - A COURSE FOR BEGINNER COACHES. It's fun, easy to follow and shows beginner coaches how to set up training, what drills to use and lots of other useful tips for volunteers coaching kids soccer.* **Search this link //bit.ly/kidscoachingcourse or head to Udemy.com and search "Chris King kids soccer course".**

2. Provide Clear Roles and Training:

Define each assistant's responsibilities to avoid confusion.

Example: "You'll handle warm-ups and assist with passing drills, while I'll focus on the small sided game setup."

Offer basic training or share resources, like videos or handouts - or books such as this :) - on kids soccer coaching techniques.

Tip: Run a "mini clinic" before (or during) the season to show assistants how to set up cones, demonstrate drills, and manage small groups. It can be for parents and volunteers of other teams as well, not just yours.

3. Encourage Collaboration:

Encourage teamwork among coaching staff by regularly discussing practice plans and game strategies. This way they feel a part of it all.

Example: "Next practice, let's split the team into two groups—I'll work on shooting, and you can run a dribbling relay drill."

Check in with assistants to ensure they feel comfortable in their roles and provide feedback.

Tip: Recognise their efforts publicly, like saying, "Coach Sarah did a fantastic job running the warm-up today – let's all give her a high five!"

4. Show Gratitude:

Thank your assistants regularly for their support.

Example: "I couldn't have managed substitutions without your help today—thank you!"

At the end of the season, give small tokens of appreciation, like personalised thank-you cards or team photos signed by the players.

3. Managing Parent Expectations

1. Be Transparent About Playing Time:

Explain your approach to playing time during the parent meeting. In my experience, equal playing time is the best way to go, no matter what the players skill level.

The parents with children with more advanced skills may want their children to get more game time. But at such a young age in grassroots football, it is all about the children's enjoyment and **making sure each and every child enjoys the experience.**

Example: "Everyone will get equal playing time during practices and games. My goal is for each player to experience different positions and develop their skills."

Stick to your plan and communicate any necessary changes promptly.

Tip: If a player's time is reduced due to injury or absence, discuss this with their parents privately to avoid misunderstandings.

2. Address Concerns Proactively:

Be open to feedback but set boundaries for when and how concerns can be raised.

Example: "Feel free to approach me after practice if you have questions—game days can be hectic, so let's save non-urgent discussions for later."

3. Keep the focus on the child's development rather than comparisons with teammates.

This is a big one. Children develop at different rates so make sure you don't compare one against other more developed and skilled players. And just because they aren't in the top couple of players at Under 7s doesn't mean they can't be the best player by the time they're playing in the under 12's team.

Sam Mitchell, of the AFL team Hawthorn FC, was overlooked constantly as a young player due to his size and speed. But he became one of the best players in the league and won multiple Premierships through practice and not giving up.

Tip: Reassure parents that every player develops at their own pace and emphasise the importance of patience and persistence.

4. Encourage a Positive Sideline Atmosphere:

Remind parents to cheer for effort and teamwork rather than focusing solely on winning.

Example: "Let's support all the players today with positive encouragement—comments like 'Great pass!' or 'Nice effort!' go a long way."

Address overly critical or disruptive behaviour politely but firmly.

Tip: Say, "Let's keep the focus on encouraging the kids—they're doing their best out there!"

5. Balance Team Needs with Individual Goals:

Find ways to align individual players' aspirations with the team's objectives.

Example: "Mark loves scoring goals, so let's also work on his passing so he can set up teammates for scoring opportunities."

Celebrate both team achievements and individual milestones to keep everyone motivated.

Tip: Highlight a mix of contributions, such as "Jason's great save kept us in the game, and Sarah's pass led to our goal!"

4. Additional Tips for Parent and Volunteer Engagement

Create a Volunteer Schedule: Divide responsibilities among parents to avoid burnout. For example, assign snack duty, carpool organisation, or game day setup on a rotating basis.

Build a Supportive Community: Encourage parents to support one another by sharing resources, like practice tips or carpool options.

Keep Things Fun: Add light-hearted elements, like a "Parents vs. Kids" game at the end of each month or the season, to build positive memories.

CONCLUSION

By building strong relationships with parents and volunteers, you create an environment that **helps the children thrive**. Communicating with the parents and volunteers, thanking them and including everyone where possible helps contribute to the team's success.

15

AGE APPROPRIATE COACHING TECHNIQUES

Topics covered in "AGE APPROPRIATE COACHING TECHNIQUES"

1. **Understanding Developmental Stages**
2. **Adapting Drills and Games to Suit Different Ages**
3. **Balancing Fun with Skill-Building**
4. **Additional Tips for Age-Appropriate Coaching**

Understanding the developmental stages of young soccer players, adapting drills and games to suit their abilities, and finding the right balance between fun and skill-building are essential for creating a positive soccer experience. Here's how to tailor your coaching approach for kids aged 5 to 10.

1. Understanding Developmental Stages

Ages 5-6:

At this stage, kids are just beginning to develop basic motor skills and coordination. Their attention spans are short, and they thrive in imaginative, playful settings.

Example: Use storytelling in drills, like pretending green cones are "trees" and the yellow cone is a "treasure" they must dribble through the forest to find.
   Tip: Focus on individual skills like dribbling and simple passing rather than tactical concepts.

Example: Introduce "Treasure Hunt," where players dribble their ball to collect cones as "treasures." At the end of each round, get each player to tell you how many pieces of treasure they found! See if they can get more on their next round.
   Additional Tip: Use plenty of praise and enthusiasm to encourage participation.

Additional Example: Play "Ball Collectors," where kids race to collect balls from a circle and dribble them back to a designated zone or to shoot into mini goals.
   Additional Tip: Add a story element, like "help the Aliens" to make it more engaging. They must get the Aliens (balls) and get them to their space ship (the mini goals).

Encourage exploration and creativity without emphasising strict rules.
   Example: "Try using both feet to dribble today—let's see what works best for you!"

Ages 7-8:

Here are some key characteristics of 7–8 year olds:

Improved Coordination and Motor Skills:

Kids at this age begin to show better balance, agility, and coordination, allowing them to execute more complex soccer moves like controlled dribbling, passing, and shooting.

Example: You may notice they can dribble around cones or teammates with more precision than younger kids.

Short Attention Spans:

They can concentrate on tasks but may lose focus quickly if activities are repetitive or unengaging.

Tip: Use short, dynamic drills and rotate activities every 10–15 minutes to maintain interest.

Increased Social Awareness:

Kids are more aware of their teammates and start to understand the importance of teamwork.

Tip: Introduce basic concepts of passing and positioning to help them learn how to work as a team. Use a drill set up like positions on a game day that works on passing from the backline to the midfield. Or from the goalkeeper to the backline.

Eagerness to Learn:

They are curious, eager to improve, and enjoy positive feedback.

Tip: Praise effort, not just results. For example, "Great technique with your shot Johnny!" instead of focusing only on scoring.

Coaching Tips for Ages 7–8

At this age, kids are ready to develop their technical soccer skills, but they need lots of repetition in a fun, supportive environment.

Focus on Fundamentals:

Dribbling: Encourage them to use both feet and keep the ball close while moving.

Drill: Set up a zig-zag cone course for dribbling practice. Time them and encourage improvement. Add a playful element like pretending they're "racing" to escape a monster.

Passing: Teach how to use the inside of the foot for accuracy.

Drill: Have pairs pass the ball through a gate (two cones) from different distances and reduce the width as they improve.

Shooting: Emphasise striking the ball with the laces if they are going for power. Or the inside of the foot if they are going for accuracy.

Game: Play "Knock the Cones" where they aim at cones placed in the goal. Award points for each cone knocked down.

Incorporate Small-Sided Games:

Play 3v3 or 4v4 games to give kids more touches on the ball and help them understand basic teamwork and basic positioning without the complexity of full-sized matches.

I'm a big exponent of playing 3v3, 4v4 mini games as often as possible. In these mini games, they have to adjust to lots of different aspects of soccer: Players are constantly changing positions, moving from attack to defence, plus there is lots of angled passing and getting into space to help teammates out.

Example: Set up a mini game with two small goals and encourage players to spread out and pass instead of crowding the ball.

Encourage Decision-Making:

At this stage, kids are ready to start learning when to dribble, pass, or shoot. Simple **decision-making exercises** can help develop their soccer IQ.

Drill Example: Play a modified 2v1 game where a defender tries to stop two attackers. This encourages players to decide when to pass or take the shot themselves.

Tip: Ask questions like, "Why did you choose to dribble instead of pass?" This encourages them to think critically about their actions.

Keep It Fun and Engaging:
Fun should always be at the heart of your sessions for 7 to 8 year olds. Imaginative games not only teach skills but also keep kids coming back to training with smiles on their faces.

Game Example: In "Pirate Soccer," players dribble to find hidden treasure (cones or objects) scattered around the field. Add golden (yellow) cones under coloured cones for bonus points.

Tip: Rotate activities often and use themes that kids can relate to, like superheroes or adventurers, to keep their enthusiasm high.

Teach Basic Team Concepts:
Start introducing positional play by showing how defenders, midfielders, and attackers work together. Keep it simple and avoid rigid formations.

While tactical play isn't the focus yet, this is a great time to introduce the basics of teamwork and positioning.

Tip: Use simple language like "stay wide" or "support your teammate when they have the ball" to help them understand spacing and movement but without overloading them with tactics.

Drill Example: In a 4v4 game, assign one player as the "helper" whose job is to always support the ball carrier by staying in a good position to receive a pass.

Ages 9–10:

Children aged 9–10 are transitioning into a more advanced stage of physical, cognitive, and social development. At this age, players are more capable of understanding structured concepts, improving technical skills, and collaborating with teammates. They also begin to develop stronger physical abilities and endurance.

Plus they start developing a competitive spirit, making it a great time to introduce more tactical elements while keeping sessions fun and engaging.

Start discussing positioning and teamwork in simple terms.

Tip: Incorporate small-sided games (e.g., 4v4, 5v5) to teach positioning, communication, and decision-making.

Example: "Let's work on creating triangles for passing options—think about how you can always give your teammate with the ball two choices."
    Tip: Add defenders to simulate real-game situations.

Additional Example: Introduce "Team Challenges," where players work together to achieve a shared goal, like completing a sequence of passes.
    Additional Tip: Use scenarios, like "breaking a defensive line," to encourage strategic thinking.

Key Characteristics of 9–10-Year-Olds

1. Improved Physical Abilities:
    Kids at this age have greater strength, endurance, and coordination, enabling them to perform more advanced soccer techniques like accurate passing over longer distances, harder shots, and quicker changes of direction.
    Example: They can now attempt longer, lofted passes to teammates.

2. Increased Cognitive Skills:

They can grasp more complex instructions and think critically about their decisions on the field. **They begin to anticipate the actions of teammates and opponents.**

Tip: Introduce drills that encourage tactical thinking, such as 3v2 attacking scenarios where 3 players must decide the best way to score versus 2 defenders.

3. Understanding of Teamwork and Positions:

Players start to understand specific roles on the field and how teamwork contributes to success. **They are better at staying in position and supporting their teammates.**

Tip: Use basic formations in small-sided games and emphasize the importance of spacing and communication.

4. Increased Competitive Spirit:

Many kids become more focused on winning, which can be a motivator but may also lead to frustration. It's essential to strike a balance between competitiveness and personal development.

Tip: Reinforce the importance of effort and learning over results. For example, praise a player for making a smart pass even if their team loses the game.

5. Social Growth and Peer Interaction:

Friendships and team dynamics become increasingly important. Kids are more sensitive to criticism but respond well to encouragement and recognition.

Tip: Encourage a positive team culture where players celebrate each other's successes and support one another after mistakes.

Coaching Tips for Ages 9–10
1. Refining Technical Skills:

Build on the basics they've already learned and challenge them to refine their skills with more precision and consistency.

Dribbling: Teach changes of speed and direction using moves like step-overs and body feints.
   Drill Example: Set up a slalom course with cones and time each player as they dribble through it. Encourage them to beat their personal best.

Passing: Focus on accuracy, weight, and timing. Introduce passing drills that involve movement.
   Drill Example: A triangle passing drill where players must pass and follow their ball to the next cone.

Shooting: Emphasize aiming for the corners of the goal and striking the ball cleanly.
   Drill Example: "Hit the Corners" where players aim to hit specific targets in the goal.

2. Introduce Tactical Concepts:
   Begin teaching basic tactics like spacing, support, and decision-making in attack and defence.
   Example: Explain how to create passing triangles by staying in positions where teammates can pass to them easily. Make sure players don't 'hide' behind an opposition player. Encourage them to get in the line of sight (also called a passing lane) so they can receive a pass from their teammate if needed.
   Drill Example: Play a 4v2 possession game where the team of 4 works to keep the ball away from 2 defenders. This builds awareness of movement and passing options.

An overload of players, like this 4v2 drill is called a rondo. I can't encourage you enough as a coach to use Rondos where ever possible at training, especially for older children, youth and adult players. Rondos work on touch, fitness, weight of pass, awareness, quick feet, plus so much more. Plus players love them! They can be played in small areas and take very little to set up.

I have two books on Rondos (Soccer Rondos Volume 1 and 2) on Amazon or search "Chris King Soccer Rondo" and you'll find them.

3. Small-Sided Games for Learning:

Use 5v5 or 7v7 games to help players practice teamwork and positioning in a controlled environment.

Tip: Pause games occasionally to discuss decisions players made and what they could do differently next time.

Example: Add constraints like "only one touch" or "the team must make three passes before shooting" to encourage creativity and teamwork.

4. Encourage Decision-Making Under Pressure:

At this age, kids can handle situations where they need to think quickly and adapt. Drills should simulate game scenarios.

Drill Example: A 2v1 attacking drill where the attacker with the ball must decide whether to pass to their teammate or take on the defender. Rotate roles frequently to give all players practice.

Tip: Ask players why they made certain choices, like dribbling instead of passing, to develop their soccer IQ.

5. Balance Fun with Competition:

Kids love games, but many also enjoy the challenge of competing. Create activities that incorporate both.

Game Example: Play "King of the Ring" where players dribble within a small area and try to knock other players' balls out while keeping control of their own. This teaches ball control under pressure.

6. Build Team Spirit and Communication:

Reinforce the importance of working together as a team. Use activities that require collaboration and communication.

Drill Example: In a passing relay, players must work together to pass the ball down the field as quickly as possible.

Tip: Celebrate team milestones, like keeping two clean sheets in a row or showing great teamwork during a match.

Examples of Effective Drills

1. Give and Go:

- Set up a line of cones. Players practice passing to a teammate, running past a cone, and receiving the ball back on the other side. This teaches quick passing and movement off the ball.

2. Attack vs. Defence:

- Set up a small-sided game where 3 attackers face 2 defenders. The attackers work together to score while the defenders try to clear the ball. Rotate roles frequently.

3. Knock Over the Flag Soccer:

- Divide players into two teams. Each team has a "flag" (a cone or pole) they must protect while trying to knock over the other team's flag. This adds a fun tactical element to practice.

Key Takeaways

- For 9–10 year olds, focus on refining skills, introducing tactical concepts, and encouraging decision-making during play.
- Small-sided games are critical for reinforcing teamwork, positioning, and communication.
- Balance competition with fun and ensure all players feel valued and supported.

By understanding the developmental needs of this age group, you can help players not only improve their skills but also develop a deeper love and understanding of the game!

2. Adapting Drills and Games to Suit Different Ages

Ages 5–6:

Dribbling Drills:

Focus on ball control with fun, creative exercises.

Example: "Red Light, Green Light," where players dribble on green and stop on red.

Tip: Add a "Yellow Light" to encourage slow, controlled dribbling.

Additional Example: Play "Follow the Leader," where players mimic the coach's dribbling moves.

Additional Tip: Add simple skills, like toe taps, to introduce coordination.

Passing Drills:

Keep passing simple and focus on technique.

Example: Partner passing in a small grid with cones as goals.

Tip: Use larger goals/gates for beginners to boost confidence.

Additional Tip: Add movement by having players jog slowly as they pass.

Shooting Drills:

Focus on fun, encouraging players to kick toward the goal without worrying about technique.

Example: "Goalie Monster," where the coach acts as the monster and kids shoot to score goals and "defeat" the monster.

Additional Example: Play "Colour Goals," where players aim at specific coloured targets in the goal called out by the coach.

Additional Tip: Reward effort and creativity with applause or high-fives.

Ages 7–8:

Dribbling Drills:
Introduce obstacles to improve control and agility.
Example: Set up cones and challenge players to dribble around them without touching the cones.
Tip: Add variation by calling out different dribbling techniques, like using only the left foot or sole rolls.

Passing Drills:
Introduce target-based drills to improve accuracy.
Example: "Passing Gates," where pairs pass the ball through cone gates and move to the next set. Reduce or widen the gates as you see fit.

Shooting Drills:
Teach basic shooting techniques like planting the non-kicking foot and following through with the striking leg.
Example: Set up small goals and challenge players to shoot from different angles.
Additional Example: Play "Dribble and Shot", where players take turns shooting after a quick dribble.
Additional Tip: Add time pressure to encourage decisive shooting.

Ages 9–10:
Dribbling Drills:
Add defensive pressure to simulate game scenarios.
Example: "1v1 Battles," where players try to dribble past a defender to score in a mini-goal.
Tip: Rotate defenders frequently to keep everyone engaged.
Additional Example: Play "Escape the Defender," where players dribble away from a trailing defender for a set time (30 seconds to 1 minute). This helps attackers practise body feints, step overs, shoulder drops, quick direction changes etc to try and lose their defender.
Additional Tip: Use zones to give players clear targets for escaping. For example, can they reach an end zone and stop their ball before the defender

enters it.

Passing Drills:
  Incorporate movement and decision-making.
  Example: "Pass and Move," where players must pass to a teammate and then run to a new space, calling to receive the next pass.
  Additional Example: Play "Chain Passing," where players form a line and pass down the chain while moving. This encourages them to turn with the ball, communicate and be aware of their surroundings. Multiple balls can be going at once if you have large numbers.
  Additional Tip: Encourage calling out names to improve communication.
  Additional Example: Run "Triangle Pass Challenge," focusing on dynamic movement and angles. This helps with receiving the ball at different angles as well as passing at different angles and weighting the pass correctly.

Shooting Drills:
  Add more advanced elements like one-touch shooting or shooting under pressure.
  Example: "Quick Fire," where players receive a pass and shoot quickly before a defender closes in.
  Additional Example: Control the ball at different heights before taking a shot. The coach or the player in front can serve the ball at different heights and speeds so players become adept at controlling.

4. Small-Sided Games:
Adapt the size of the field and number of players to suit their developmental stage.
  Ages 5–6: play 3v3/4v4 with no goalkeepers to maximize touches.
  Ages 7-8: play 4v4/5v5 with no goalkeepers but introduce passing restrictions before shooting (ie 3 passes before you can shoot).
  Ages 9–10: play 5v5/6v6 with keepers to introduce more structure.

3. Balancing Fun with Skill-Building

1. Keep It Playful:

Use games and themes to make practices engaging and enjoyable.

Incorporate silly challenges, like dribbling with one hand on their head, singing their favourite song, or hopping on one foot during warm-ups.

Example: Play "Soccer Bowling," where players aim to knock down cones with their shots.

Tip: Use varying distances to challenge players of different skill levels. Or get them to perform a skill/trick before trying to knock the cone down.

2. Use Progressions:

Start with simple activities and gradually increase the complexity as players improve.

Example: Begin with stationary passing, then progress to passing while moving, and finally add a defender.

Tip: Ensure drills remain achievable to maintain confidence.

3. Celebrate Small Wins:

Recognize and praise improvement, effort, and creativity.

Example: "I loved how you tried that step-over move today—great effort, and it almost worked! I bet next time you'll trick them."

Tip: Create a "Skill of the Day" challenge and reward players for attempting it during practice or games.

4. Incorporate Friendly Competition:

Add team challenges and points systems to keep players motivated.

Example: Award points for completed passes, goals, or defensive stops in small-sided games. Tally the points as you go and see which team has the most every 5 minutes.

Tip: Emphasize teamwork by awarding bonus points for assists or communication.

5. Rotate Activities Often:

Change drills every 10–15 minutes to keep kids engaged and avoid boredom.

Example: Transition from a dribbling relay to a quick shooting game, then end with a small-sided scrimmage.

Tip: Use music or countdowns to signal transitions and maintain energy levels.

Additional Example: Set up multiple stations focusing on different skills, like shooting, dribbling, and passing. Players can rotate through to a different station every 10 minutes.

Additional Tip: Let players choose their favourite station for the last few minutes of practice.

Additional Example: Create a "Mystery Station" with surprise activities to keep interest high. Some examples may be juggling, trying a trick, soccer golf (passing to an object in the least amount of passes possible) or soccer tennis (set up cones along the halfway line of a rectangle and players kick the ball over the cones and have to kick it back over before the ball bounces twice).

Note: For my older teams, I always have a couple of soccer rectangles set up before training. So any players that arrive early can have a game against each other. It improves touch and is a great way to lightly warm up and see who is the best soccer tennis player.

4. Additional Tips for Age-Appropriate Coaching

Be Patient: Younger players will need more repetition and encouragement to grasp new skills. Make sure to celebrate effort over perfection.

Ask for Feedback: Check in with players about their favourite activities and adapt practices accordingly.

Model Positivity: Show enthusiasm and energy to keep kids motivated and excited to learn.

CONCLUSION

By understanding the needs of each age group, adapting drills to match their abilities, and balancing fun with skill-building, you'll create an environment where players develop their skills and love for the game. Tailoring your training sessions to be age appropriate ensures that every child feels valued and motivated to improve.

16

MASTER SOCCER SKILLS AT HOME

Topics covered in "MASTER SOCCER SKILLS AT HOME"

1. **Simple Drills for Home Practice**
2. **Fun Games to Improve Individual Skills**
3. **Encouraging Consistency**

Practising at home is a fantastic way for young players to improve their skills, build confidence, and develop a love for the game. I used to love kicking the ball against the couch, juggle a small skills ball when I walked across the street to my mates place or just go out in the backyard and set up an obstacle of sticks and pot plants to dribble around. Not to mention that my dad and I used to have a 15 minute game up and own the hallway before tea every night with a tennis ball. All this extra time spent with a ball at my feet immensely helped my skills and confidence on the ball.

By keeping exercises simple, fun, and consistent, kids can see real progress while enjoying their time with the ball.

1. Simple Drills for Home Practice

1. Wall Passing:

Players pass the ball against a wall and control the rebound.

Example: "Try to hit a specific spot on the wall and control the ball with different parts of your foot when it comes back."

Tip: Add variety by alternating between left and right feet and increasing the distance from the wall.

Progression: Challenge kids to complete 10 passes in a row without letting the ball stop.

Variation: Use targets marked on the wall (like taped or chalked circles) for accuracy practice. Award more points for hitting smaller targets.

Advanced Idea: Combine wall passing with a movement drill. After each pass, the player runs or dribbles to a cone and back before the next pass.

> *Bonus tip: You can buy a soccer rebounder board from the internet. They aren't cheap but they are a great way for your child to be able to practice anywhere (or to use for your team at training). You can get ones that use pins to keep it in the grass and others that come with little sand bags to fill with sand to weight them down so you can use them on artificial surfaces. If your child shows a real interest in practising at home it is a great investment. Just search "soccer rebounder board".*

2. Dribbling Challenges:

Create a mini obstacle course using cones, poles, water bottles, the garden hose or shoes.

Example: "Weave through the cones as quickly as you can without hitting them."

Tip: Time each run and encourage kids to beat their previous score.

Variation: Add challenges like dribbling with their non-dominant foot or performing a specific move (e.g., a step-over) at each obstacle.

Bonus Tip: Incorporate household items like chairs for tighter turns or passing under. Or set up two parallel courses for races with a sibling or friend.

Fun Twist: Add a "gate" made of two objects, where players must dribble through to complete the course. Or a small circle where players must stop the ball in to improve their ball control.

Additional Tip: Encourage creativity by letting players design their own dribbling courses.

Bonus Drill: "Volcanoes" is an easy drill to set up. Spread cones/objects randomly in a tight area. The player must simply dribble around the area using different parts of their feet and doing different turns, avoiding the objects. Go for a minute and see how many volcanoes they hit. Can they get through a minute without hitting a volcano? Can they get faster? Can they use only their non-preferred foot? Can they do sole rolls going backwards? There are endless dribbling skills that can be performed with this drill.

Watch as their confidence and skill level improves out of sight the more time they spend practising at home!

3. Passing Drills:

Practice passing accuracy with household items. Outside the house can you pass through a gate? Against a wall? Between two trees? Between a two poles/sticks? Nutmeg the dog?

Inside the house can you pass under a chair? Do a one-two with the back of the couch?

Soccer is a great sport that you don't need a partner to practice most of the skills. Use your imagination and you'll find plenty of ways to practice passing outside or inside your house.

Example: Use "Bucket Target," where kids aim passes into a laundry basket or bucket.

Tip: Gradually increase the distance as accuracy improves.

Additional Example: Try "Pass Back Challenge," where a parent or sibling returns passes to encourage quick reactions.

Additional Tip: Incorporate non-dominant foot passes to enhance overall skill.

> **Note:** *Sometimes when practising inside the house it can be slippery just wearing regular socks when dribbling or doing stationary skills. There are grip socks that you can buy online or from your local sports store that help reduce slipping. They are easy to find and quite popular now. Just search "soccer grip skill socks".*

4. Juggling Practice:

Teach kids to keep the ball in the air using their feet, thighs, or head. Juggling helps work on touch and control so it is a great skill to practice.

Example: For beginners - "Start with one juggle and catch, then try for two in a row and catch."

Tip: Use a smaller or lighter ball, like a tennis ball, for added difficulty and fun. And the opposite for beginners: Use a balloon to start with or a soft, squeezy ball.

Progression: Challenge players to alternate touches between their feet or add thigh-to-foot combinations.

Fun Twist: Turn it into a game by counting how many consecutive juggles they can achieve. Set a "family record" to break.

Advanced Idea: Add a creative element by asking kids to include tricks like a "rainbow flick" after juggling five times. I've never been able to do a rainbow flick.

Step-by-Step Guide on Juggling for Beginners:
  1. Start with Holding It in Your Hands and Drop:

- Hold the ball in both hands.
- Drop it and try to kick it back up with one foot.
- Let it bounce before catching it again.

2. Focus on One Kick:

- Practice kicking the ball once and catching it.
- Encourage controlled, gentle kicks using the top of the foot (laces area).

3. Progress to Consecutive Kicks:

- Try kicking the ball twice before catching it. It's ok to bounce in between while learning to juggle.
- Gradually build up to more kicks without catching.

4. Use Both Feet:

- Encourage using both feet so children develop better balance and control.

5. Keep the Ball Low:

- Emphasise small, controlled touches to keep the ball low and easier to manage. They will be tempted to kick it hard and high but make sure to tell them just to do small, low kicks/touches.

Tips for Success:

- **Keep it Fun:** Make it a game! Count how many juggles they can do or set small challenges.
- **Start with a Softer Ball:** A softer or slightly under-inflated ball can make learning easier.
- **Use a Balloon or Beach Ball:** For very young kids, start with a balloon to develop coordination before moving to a soccer ball.
- **Celebrate Small Wins:** Praise effort and improvement, not perfection.
- **Practice Often:** Short, regular practice sessions work better than long ones.

Key Coaching Advice:

- Be patient and positive.
- Let kids explore and experiment with the ball.
- Juggling improves gradually, so keep it light-hearted and fun!

5. Target Shooting:

Set up a small goal or mark targets on a wall with tape.

Example: "Try to hit the top corners of the goal or specific spots on the wall."

Tip: Award points for accuracy, like 3 points for the top corners and 1 point for hitting the centre.

Variation: Use different coloured targets and call out colours for kids to aim for mid-drill. You can hang different coloured bibs in the top corners of a goal or place different coloured cones in the bottom corners.

Fun Game: Introduce "Target Knockout," where players try to knock down plastic cups or small objects placed on the wall or goal frame.

Advanced Idea: Incorporate movement into the drill, like receiving a pass from a partner before taking the shot.

Additional Example: Set up "Moving Target," where a family member moves a target for kids to aim at. Can they strike a ball and hit a broom as you walk along with it?

Additional Tip: Encourage players to shoot quickly after receiving a pass to mimic game situations.

6. First Touch Practice:

Kick the ball against a wall and practice controlling it with different parts of the body (inside of the foot, thigh, chest, etc).

Example: "Control the ball with one touch and pass it back."

Tip: Use a partner to toss or kick the ball for more variety.

Additional Example: "Stationary Traps," where kids stop a rolling ball with the inside or sole of their foot.

Additional Tip: Roll the ball at varying speeds, heights and angles for added challenge.

Variation: Add movement by controlling the ball and dribbling to a cone before passing it back.

Challenge: Use different surfaces to simulate unpredictable rebounds. Practice on bumpy ground and in the wet. Plus can they keep concentration while being sprayed with the hose? :)

Advanced Idea: Include a follow-up action, like taking a shot on a mini-goal after controlling the ball with their first touch.

7. Speed Dribbling:

Mark a start and finish line and time players as they dribble as fast as possible without losing control.

Example: "See if you can beat your own record by half a second!"

Tip: Use markers to create zigzag patterns for more advanced challenges.

Variation: Add a "gate" halfway through the course where players must perform a move, like a pull-back or step-over, before continuing.

2. Fun Games to Improve Individual Skills

1. Around the World:

Place cones to form a circle and challenge the player to dribble around each one as quickly as possible.

Variation: Change directions or require specific moves at each cone, like a drag-back or a step-over.

Tip: Add a timer to encourage speed or a competitive edge when practising with a sibling.

2. Goalie Wars:

Set up two small goals a few yards apart and have players take turns being the striker (shooting) and the goalkeeper (saving).

Example: "Score as many goals as you can in 30 seconds!"

Tip: Use a softer ball indoors or move the goals farther apart outdoors for more of a challenge.

Variation: Add "power shots" by encouraging players to use their laces for more powerful kicks.

3. 1-Minute Challenges:

Create timed tasks to motivate players to push themselves.

Example: "How many successful passes can you make against the wall in one minute?"

Tip: Track scores (buy a note pad to write daily scores in) and encourage kids to beat their personal best each day/week.

Variation: Add creative challenges like "How many toe taps can you do in 1 minute with your eyes closed?"

4. Skill Stations:

Set up multiple small activity stations (e.g., passing, dribbling, juggling) and rotate every few minutes.

Example: "Spend 2 minutes at each station, focusing on your technique. Rest for 30 seconds after each station."

Tip: Add music to keep energy levels high and make transitions fun!

Variation: Include fun bonus stations like "ball tricks" or "goal celebrations."

5. Cone Knockdown:

Place cones at varying distances and challenge players to knock them down with accurate passes or shots.

Example: "From this spot try and hit as many cones as you can in 1 minute!"

Tip: Award more points for cones placed farther away or in trickier positions.

Advanced Variation: Combine cone knockdowns with dribbling by requiring players to dribble around a cone before taking their shot. This way they get used to passing when moving which is more match realistic.

Additional Tip: Set time limits for each round to encourage fast decision-making.

3. Encouraging Consistency

1. Set a Routine:
Encourage players to practice at the same time each day to build a habit.
Example: "Practice for 15 minutes after school or before dinner (or both!)."
Tip: Create a calendar or chart to track daily progress.
Bonus: Include "family challenge days" where parents or siblings join in the routine.

2. Make It Social:
Pair up with a sibling, friend, or parent for extra motivation.
Example: "Play a passing game with a family member and see how many passes you can complete in a row."
Tip: Turn drills into friendly competitions to add excitement.
Variation: Introduce team games like "keep away" or "tag" to practice possession skills. Young kids through to older adults enjoy a good game of tag!

3. Incorporate Challenges and Rewards:
Set achievable goals and celebrate when they're reached.
Example: "Once you master 5 juggles, we'll record a video to share with your coach!"
Tip: Use small rewards like stickers, extra playtime or they get to choose the Sunday night movie as incentives.
Bonus: Celebrate larger milestones with a fun outing or a new piece of soccer gear.
Additional Example: "Penalty Kick Duel," where players take turns shooting penalties against each other.
Additional Tip: Add playful stakes, like choosing the next snack or who has to wash up, to make it more fun.

4. Keep It Fun:
Emphasize enjoyment over winning and perfection.

Example: "Pretend you're in a World Cup final while practising your shots!"

Variation: Add themed days like "Freestyle Friday," where players invent and perform their own soccer tricks.

CONCLUSION

Practising soccer at home can be a lot of fun! Whether kids are working on simple drills, playing games, or just kicking the ball around, every little bit helps them improve. The more they enjoy it, the more they'll want to keep practising.

Keep it light and exciting. Celebrate their progress, no matter how small, and let them explore and have fun with the game. By making practice playful, you'll help them build skills and fall in love with soccer even more.

> *If you'd like a free book, 50 TIPS ON HOW TO COACH A CHILDREN'S SOCCER TEAM – Ages 3 to 6 is available on Amazon permanently free.*
>
> *Plus head to my website www.chriskingsoccercoach.com and enter your email for a free PDF copy of a soccer coaching book.*
>
> ***Thank You for Reading!*** *If this book has been valuable so far, please consider leaving a review on Amazon. Your feedback helps spread the word and lets other new coaches find my books.*
>   ***USA REVIEW LINK:*** *https://www.Amazon.com/review*
>   ***UK REVIEW LINK:*** *https://www.Amazon.co.uk/review/create-review?&asin=B0D48YQ1DH*

Special Offer – Online Kids Coaching Course

As a reader of this book, you can get my *Coaching Kids Soccer* course on Udemy at a discounted price.

    ☞ Use this link to access the discount: https://rebrand.ly/kidscourse

17

END OF SEASON WRAP UP AND REFLECTION

Topics covered in "END OF SEASON WRAP UP and REFLECTION"

1. **Celebrating Progress and Achievements**
2. **Hosting an Awards Day or Fun Event**
3. **Reflecting on Lessons Learned for Future Seasons**

The end of the season is an opportunity to celebrate progress and reflect on achievements. By thoughtfully wrapping up the season, you create a positive end to the season and inspire players to continue on their soccer journey.

1. Celebrating Progress and Achievements

1. Highlight Individual Growth

Acknowledge how each player has improved in their skills, teamwork, and confidence.

Example: "Kate, your dribbling has come so far since the start of the season—you've become such a creative player!"

Tip: Create a "Before and After" chart or slide show, showing players' progress in specific skills, like passing accuracy or juggling.

Additional Example: Use practice photos or short video clips to demonstrate visible improvements. If you don't have the technical skills or time, is there another parent that could put together some photos or videos?

Additional Tip: Share written feedback with players of their improvement over the season to provide a keepsake they can look back on.

2. Celebrate Team Milestones

Recognise moments where the team demonstrated growth, like achieving their first clean sheet or completing five consecutive passes in a game.

Example: "Remember our game against the Riverside Rats? That was the first time we scored from a set play—awesome teamwork!"

Tip: Create a "Season Highlights" poster or digital collage with photos and key achievements.

Additional Example: Compile a list of "Top 10 Moments" and share it during the final team meeting or event.

Additional Tip: Highlight contributions from every player to ensure everyone feels valued.

3. Encourage Positive Peer Recognition

Let players share what they appreciated about their teammates.

Example: "I liked how Chris always cheered for us, even when we were behind."

Tip: Organise a "Compliment Circle" where each player gives and receives positive feedback.

Additional Example: Pass around a "Team Journal" towards the end of the season for players to write notes of encouragement to each other. Then display these notes on a "Wall of Encouragement" during the final event.

2. Hosting an Awards Day or Fun Event

1. Plan a Team Party:
Host a celebration to reflect on the season and thank everyone involved.
Example: Organise a picnic or pizza party at a local park or field.
Tip: Incorporate light-hearted activities, like a parents-vs-kids game.

Additional Example: Include a "Skills Carnival" with stations like shooting challenges, dribbling courses, and juggling contests.
Additional Tip: Use trophies or certificates for participation to make the event more special.

2. Distribute Awards:
Recognise players with fun and meaningful awards.
Example: "Most Improved Dribbler," "Best Team Spirit," or "Defensive Dynamo." Ensure every player receives an award that reflects their unique contributions.

Additional Example: Create themed awards, like "Energizer Bunny" for the most tireless player or "Quiet Leader" for a shy but impactful teammate. Include light-hearted categories like "Funniest Goal Celebration" to add humour.

3. Involve Parents and Volunteers:
Use the event to thank everyone who supported the team.
Example: Present certificates of appreciation to assistant coaches, team managers, and parent volunteers.
Tip: Share a slide-show or video montage that highlights parents cheering on the sidelines and helping at practices.

Additional Example: Include a "Volunteer Spotlight" segment where players thank specific adults for their contributions.
Additional Tip: End the event with a group photo to commemorate the

season.

3. Reflecting on Lessons Learned for Future Seasons

1. Gather Player Feedback:

Ask players what they enjoyed most and what they'd like to improve next season. This can help you to improve as a coach.

Example: "What was your favourite drill or game this year, and why?"

Tip: Use a fun survey or comment box to collect responses.

Additional Example: Host a "Team Huddle Reflection," where players share ideas for future goals. Encourage them to set personal goals, like "I want to score with my left foot next season."

2. Review Team Goals:

Reflect on whether the team met the objectives set at the beginning of the season.

Example: "At the start of the season, we aimed to improve our passing. I'm proud to say we've come a long way!". Highlight both successes and areas for continued growth in a positive tone.

3. Coach's Personal Reflection:

Take time to assess your own performance as a coach and identify areas for improvement.

Example: "Next season, I'd like to focus more on one-on-one skill development during practices."

Tip: Keep a journal throughout the season to document what worked well and what could be refined.

Additional Example: Share your reflections with assistant coaches to brainstorm ideas for improvement.

Additional Tip: Seek feedback from parents and players to gain different perspectives.

4. Prepare for Off Season Engagement:

Encourage players to stay active and practice during the off season.

Example: Provide a simple guide with fun drills and exercises they can do at home (refer back to the previous chapter on drills and skills to do at home).

Tip: Recommend local soccer camps or clinics to keep players engaged.

Additional Example: Create a "Summer Soccer Challenge" with tasks like juggling a ball 20 times or scoring in the top corner five times.

Additional Tip: Start a team WhatsApp group to share updates, tips, and encouragement during the break.

CONCLUSION

By celebrating achievements, hosting a memorable event, and reflecting on lessons learned, you'll create a positive end-of-season experience that motivates players to continue improving. A thoughtful wrap-up ensures that everyone—players, parents, and coaches—feels proud of their contributions and excited for the future.

18

OTHER SOCCER BOOKS, COURSES AND PODCASTS BY CHRIS KING

Before the last couple of chapters, I wanted to let you know about my other soccer/football coaching material.

I have lots of other kids and adult **soccer books** on Amazon, **online soccer coaching courses** on Udemy.com plus **soccer coaching Podcasts**.

Follow the links below and keep improving as a soccer coach!

AMAZON SOCCER COACHING BOOKS

Search "Chris King Amazon author page" or follow the links:
  Coaching Kids Soccer Volumes 1,2,3: //bit.ly/coachingkidssoccer
  Amazon USA: //bit.ly/socceramazonauthorpage
  Amazon UK: //bit.ly/amazonuksoccer

ONLINE SOCCER COACHING COURSES:

Visit the links below or if you're reading a paperback type in the links to go directly to the course:

HOW TO COACH KIDS SOCCER - A COURSE FOR BEGINNER COACHES: https://rebrand.ly/kidscourse

HOW TO COACH SOCCER - TRAINING SESSIONS FOR GRASSROOTS COACHES: https://rebrand.ly/adultcourse

PODCASTS:

Search "Chris King soccer podcast" or follow the links:

COACHING KIDS SOCCER PODCAST
//bit.ly/podcastkidssoccer
//bit.ly/kidspodcastapple
COACHING WALKING FOOTBALL PODCAST
//bit.ly/3OW9LP1

19

THE IMPORTANCE OF PLAY AND CREATIVITY

Topics covered in "THE IMPORTANCE of PLAY and CREATIVITY"

1. **Why Play and Creativity Matter**
2. **Ways to Incorporate Play into Training**
3. **Encouraging Creativity**

Young children learn best through playing, and soccer is no different. Encouraging creativity and play helps kids develop a love for the game, discover their strengths, and build problem solving skills on the pitch.

1. Why Play and Creativity Matter

1. **Boosts Engagement:**

Unstructured play keeps kids motivated and eager to participate. Start and finish practice with a fun activity or game to ensure players leave on a positive note.

Example: Try ending with a fun game like "Sharks and Minnows" where kids dribble to avoid being tagged, reinforcing ball control in a playful, creative setting.

2. **Encourages Problem Solving:**

Giving children the freedom to make decisions during games helps them develop soccer intelligence and decision making skills.

Tip: Avoid over-coaching during small sided games. Let players figure out how to pass, dribble, or defend on their own. As a player, you don't want to be stopped every minute to be told what to do (especially if it's to be told what you've done wrong!).

To a certain extent, just let them play - and if you must tell them something, you can always go onto the pitch and tell Johnny "Try and stay out wide" when play isn't near him and give him a high five.

Example: Set up a small sided game, adding in extra goals (have two goals at each end) and no goalkeepers. Players must figure out how to defend and score creatively.

3. **Creates Confidence:**

When kids feel free to try new moves without fear of mistakes, they gain confidence. Praise creativity, even if the move doesn't work. Celebrate the effort!

Example: If a child attempts a step-over but loses control of the ball, acknowledge their initiative for trying the move.

2. Ways to Incorporate Play into Training:

1. **Game Based Drills:**

Play small-sided games (like 3v3) where the focus is on fun and decision making, not competition. **Note:** 3v3 is a great number of players to have a small sided game. Players are constantly using different angled passes to find a free teammate, they must go from being an attacker to a defender and visa versa constantly, there are lot of 1v1s so players learn to get past a defender, plus all players get lots of touches on the ball.

Tip: Set up mini-goals without keepers instead of a standard goal with a keeper to encourage more shooting and creative play.

2. **Skill Challenges:**

Fun competitions like "Who can dribble through the cone maze the fastest?"

Tip: Also include non-competitive skill challenges where the focus is personal bests instead of winners.

3. **Themed Practices:**

Incorporate playful stories into drills. For example, "Treasure Island" where kids must protect their soccer ball (the treasure) from pirates (defenders).

Tip: Let the kids come up with their own themes and stories for some practices.

3. Encouraging Creativity

1. **Allow Kids to Invent Drills:**

Give players five minutes to design their own game or drill at the end of practice. Provide cones and let them explain their creation to the group.

2. **Rotate Leadership Roles:**

Allow kids to take turns leading warm-ups or calling out drill instructions. Assign a "captain of the day" to help with small tasks and build leadership skills.

3. **Reward Creative Thinking:**

Positive reinforcement helps build a fearless mindset.

Example: If a child attempts a back heel pass during a game, praise their effort even if it fails.

Key Tip: Balance Structure with Freedom

While structure is essential for skill development, it's equally important to give players freedom to explore and play.

Example: Set a 10-minute "free play" zone at the start of each session where kids can dribble, juggle, or pass however they choose.

CONCLUSION

By focusing on **creative play**, you'll not only help kids improve their soccer skills but also encourage a lifelong love for the sport. Keep the focus on enjoyment and making soccer a positive experience for every player.

20

PLAYER DEVELOPMENT AND LONG-TERM GROWTH

Topics covered in "PLAYER DEVELOPMENT and LONG-TERM GROWTH"

1. **Focus on Fundamentals First**
2. **Individualised Development Paths**

Coaching kids' soccer is about more than teaching immediate skills—it's about creating a long-term development mindset that helps young players grow on and off the field. Understanding how children progress through different stages can help you create a positive experience while keeping their future development in mind.

1. Focus on Fundamentals First

As mentioned numerous times during this book, at younger ages (5-10), the focus should be on mastering the basics—dribbling, passing, shooting, and ball control—while keeping it fun and accessible to all.

Tip: Break down skills into small steps. For example, when teaching dribbling, focus on using small touches with the inside of the foot before introducing changes of direction.

Example: If working on passing, start with stationary partner passing before progressing to passing while walking and eventually running.

1. The Long Game Approach:

Player development is a marathon, not a sprint. Emphasise gradual progress rather than short term results.

Tip: Reframe "mistakes" as learning moments. Encourage players to reflect on what they learned after a difficult drill or match.

Example: If a child struggles to control the ball under pressure, reassure them that it's part of the learning process and highlight how their effort is what matters.

2. Measuring Success Beyond the Scoreboard:

True development *goes beyond match results* and should focus on skill improvement, teamwork, and personal growth.

Tip: Create a "Player Progress Board" where each player sets a personal goal for the season (like improving their non-dominant foot, learning a new trick or learning a new position).

Example: Praise improvements in attitude and sportsmanship, such as helping a teammate or encouraging others during practice.

3. Building Physical Literacy:

Physical literacy is essential for young players and includes developing coordination, balance, and agility alongside soccer-specific skills.

Drill Idea: Set up an "Agility Ladder" where players walk through the ladder performing sole rolls or toe taps to combine fitness and ball control.

Tip: Encourage multi-sport participation for younger players to develop well-rounded athletic skills.

4. Growth Through Challenges:

Kids learn best when challenged appropriately. Allow them to try new positions and skills, even if it feels uncomfortable.

Tip: Rotate positions in small sided games, ensuring each player experiences different roles (goalkeeper, defence, midfield, and attack).

Example: If a player hesitates to play as a defender, explain how it helps them understand offensive strategies too (by playing in defence they can learn what works or doesn't work for the oppositions striker).

2. Individualized Development Paths

Every child develops at a different pace. Recognise progress specific to each player rather than comparing them against teammates.

CONCLUSION

Long-term player development in kids' soccer is about steady progress, patience, and focusing on fundamentals over results. By emphasising individual growth, physical literacy, and personal milestones, coaches can create a positive learning environment that helps children develop both their skills and love for the game.

Remember, the goal is not just to develop soccer players but to inspire lifelong learners who enjoy staying active and engaged in the sport.

21

FINAL THOUGHTS

THE BEGINNER'S GUIDE TO COACHING KIDS SOCCER
A Complete Resource For Parents And Volunteers
- From First Practice To Game Day -

Remember that being a great coach is about more than teaching the sport—it's about inspiring a love for the game and creating positive experiences for young players. Your guidance and encouragement can help shape their confidence and personal growth, both on and off the field.

By focusing on fun, skill development, and inclusivity, you're building a team where every child feels valued. Keep celebrating progress, stay flexible in your coaching approach, and continue learning alongside your players.

Thanks for coaching at grassroots level! You should be extremely proud of yourself.
   Keep on coaching!
   Chris King

———————-

FINAL THOUGHTS

Thank You for Reading! Please spend 2 minutes and leave a book review!

If you've got some great value from this book I would appreciate it if you could help a fellow soccer coach out and leave a review! It can just be a sentence or two.

Follow this link
USA REVIEW LINK: *https://www.Amazon.com/review*
UK REVIEW LINK: *https://www.Amazon.co.uk/review/create-review?&asin=B0D48YQ1DH*

or head to the book page on Amazon and scroll down to "WRITE A CUSTOMER REVIEW" button under the customer reviews on the left hand side.

Head to my website www.chriskingsoccercoach.com and enter your email for a free PDF copy of a coaching book.

If you'd like a free book, 50 TIPS ON HOW TO COACH A CHILDREN'S SOCCER TEAM - Ages 3 to 6 is available on Amazon permanently free.

AMAZON SOCCER COACHING BOOKS

Search "Chris King Amazon author page" or follow the links:
Coaching Kids Soccer Volumes 1,2,3: //bit.ly/coachingkidssoccer
Amazon USA: //bit.ly/socceramazonauthorpage
Amazon UK: //bit.ly/amazonuksoccer

ONLINE SOCCER COACHING COURSES HOSTED ON UDEMY.COM:

Head to Udemy.com and search "Chris King Soccer" or visit the links below. If you're reading a paperback type in the links to go directly to the course:

HOW TO COACH KIDS SOCCER - A COURSE FOR BEGINNER COACHES: https://rebrand.ly/kidscourse

HOW TO COACH SOCCER - TRAINING SESSIONS FOR GRASSROOTS COACHES: https://rebrand.ly/adultcourse

PODCASTS:

Search "Chris King soccer podcast" or follow the links:

COACHING KIDS SOCCER PODCAST

//bit.ly/podcastkidssoccer

//bit.ly/kidspodcastapple

COACHING WALKING FOOTBALL PODCAST

//bit.ly/3OW9LP1

Printed in Dunstable, United Kingdom